For nearly 30 years Richard Winter has studied and practised Buddhism and meditation at the Cambridge Buddhist Centre, and he currently teaches meditation at the Buddhist Centre for students of the Cambridge University of the Third Age. As a Professor of Education at Anglia Ruskin University, Cambridge, UK, his research was mainly concerned with helping nurses, social workers and teachers to develop reflective, critical and creative methods of working. He is currently involved as a member of a radical political campaigning group and has also been a (frustrated) semi-active member of a political party for several decades.

To meditators and democrats everywhere.

* * * * *

NOTE

The text of *How to BE the Change We Need* was complete by the beginning of 2022 and strangely enough, for most of the following year an apparently endless succession of events illustrated precisely the themes of the book – a general sense of despair about the state of our public life and also a sense that no-one knew what to do about it. However, due to unavoidable delays in the publication process, it was not possible to include references to all this in the book. At first this seemed to be unfortunate, although it did show the relevance, indeed the prescience of the book's themes. On the other hand it would have been difficult to refer to these highly controversial events without seeming to be 'taking sides'; whereas it will become clear that the aim of the book is to indicate the importance of such controversies while remaining strictly non-partisan.

Richard Winter

HOW TO BE THE CHANGE WE NEED

MEDITATION AND POLITICS

AUSTIN MACAULEY PUBLISHERS™

LONDON • CAMBRIDGE • NEW YORK • SHARJAH

A CIP catalogue record for this title is available from the British Library.

ISBN 9781398471924 (Paperback)
ISBN 9781398471931 (ePub e-book)

www.austinmacauley.com

First Published 2023
Austin Macauley Publishers Ltd®
1 Canada Square
Canary Wharf
London
E14 5AA

Many thanks to all the people who have offered support and helpful suggestions: family, friends, fellow students at the Cambridge Trirtana Buddhist Community, and students who attended the 'University of the Third Age' meditation courses at the Cambridge Buddhist Centre.

Table of Contents

Chapter One
Politics and Meditation –
Introduction and Overview

'What's wrong with us all!' I exclaim, burying my head in my hands as I read the newspapers or watch TV or listen to the radio.

I mean, what possesses British Members of Parliament (reasonably well off and most of them motivated originally, I'm sure, mainly by some sort of ideal of public service) to fiddle their expense accounts and get you and me, indirectly, to fund the extravagant redecoration of their second homes?

And what about the United States government tightening economic sanctions against impoverished countries where they disagree with the policies of the regime, and thereby preventing them from importing crucial *medical* supplies?

And then there is the resurgence of Holocaust denial and the rise to near-respectability, in some circles, of racist and quasi-fascist political attitudes and organisations. I'm thinking especially of some Eastern European countries governed by parties with a historical link to policies of collaboration with Nazi occupiers during the 1939–45 war.

And statistics showing the level of everyday violence against women, in so many parts of the world that it seems to be part of a global political and cultural norm.

A daily occurrence, hardly even news any longer, is the drowning of refugees fleeing across the Mediterranean in rubber dinghies, while European governments argue that many of them are not 'really' escaping from starvation or war or torture, and so are not covered by the United Nations Convention on Human Rights, while those rescuing them are liable to prosecution.

As I write (2021), impoverished nations are being denied access to patented Covid-19 vaccines while rich producer nations are stockpiling them. And yet everyone knows that unvaccinated populations on the other side of the world offer viruses the opportunity to mutate and thus to pose a continuing threat to us all.

Finally, to take perhaps the most familiar example: for decades governments have been holding regular international conferences where carefully worded resolutions are passed, *promising* to control global warming. Meanwhile, the polar ice cap and the glaciers continue to melt at an ever-increasing speed, Australia and Florida are racked by unprecedented forest fires, and Pacific Island states are starting to disappear under the ocean, to be followed inevitably by many of our major cities.

In each case it seems that something is so obviously wrong that if the evidence were not so clear we would find it difficult to believe. Such lack of awareness of others, such callousness, such failure to learn from the past, such blinkered incoherence, such failure to anticipate consequences, such rudimentary lack of imagination, such massive ethical failure!

Whether it boils down to hypocrisy, self-delusion or some strange form of incompetence, the occurrence (the familiarity indeed) of such events seems to indicate a collective deficiency in our political culture, creating, not surprisingly, a widespread lack of trust or confidence concerning the operation of our political institutions.

But to suggest that what is needed is a 'change of political culture' is not very helpful. Partly because 'culture' is a vague and ambiguous word that gives no indication as to what sort of actions should be undertaken and by whom and in what order. And partly, also, because what is lacking doesn't only concern our politicians: it concerns all of us, because, as individuals, we vote for them. Does this then mean that in the end the problem is simply a matter of education? (Since in practical terms it is the combined educational experiences of the individuals who make up an electorate who create the background 'culture' on which the life of politics depends.)

We could say, yes, education is indeed the key to our problems; but this is not very helpful unless we specify what *sort* of education? Because *some* sort of educational process is as old as humanity; organised schools and curricula are as old as civilisation; and so-called 'universal' education' has been widespread for well over a century. So, in many ways our current political predicament is precisely what our various educational traditions have left us with. Thus, if we are to progress from where we are, we need something radically different, which is the argument of this book: namely, let us try to introduce into all educational situations, by all the means at our disposal, the processes and practices of *meditation.*

Politics and Meditation?
"You Must Be Joking!"

No, I'm not joking – far from it; but I can understand why my friend in the local Constituency Party seemed, when I mentioned the idea, to think I was. Because the general understanding is that politics and meditation have no more in common than chalk and cheese. Politics is all about engaging in the practical decision-making required to carry on (or change) our social affairs. Whereas meditation, in contrast, may remind us of seeking an *escape* into tranquillity. Politics is action, whereas meditation is contemplation. And meditation focuses on the individual, whereas politics involves the collective – the community, even if only locally. But these are exactly the sort of simple oppositions that get in the way of what I suggest is a fruitful line of enquiry.

So let me, instead, approach the issue from two different angles. First, the well-known observation that 'the personal is political', referring to the way in which the institutions that embody our society's political assumptions (on race and gender for example) impact directly on, and are also derived from, our individual experiences. And secondly, the equally well-known phrase: "politics is the art of the possible" [1]. This is often quoted as a warning by those who think that 'decision-making' must be guided by what is already familiar, in order to avoid supposedly 'unrealistic' notions of what it is possible to change. In this way, what is familiar represents a political state of affairs that individuals need to accept as more or less fixed and unchangeable.

In contrast, as a rejoinder to both phrases, meditation might be described as *expanding our understanding* of a) what we know about our familiar reality (including ourselves) and in this way b) expanding our sense of what is possible. The dictionary describes meditation as, among other things, 'the application of the mind'. But this would of course also be a component of any form of *political action*, and from this perspective at least it is not difficult to claim some sort of political relevance for meditation. But it is the form of this relevance and the processes needed if we are to examine the *possibility of cultural change* that I wish to explore.

I am not of course suggesting that meditation can be a substitute for the other strategies for political change with which we are familiar, i.e., contesting current policies and forms of institutional life in areas such as education, welfare, policing, trade unions, taxation, immigration etc., through collective organising, protesting, campaigning, attending meetings, writing to newspapers, or donating to charities or political crowd-funding. Or, if you are a professional politician: debating policies and passing legislation. My argument, rather, is that meditation can enhance the *effectiveness* of our contribution to such activities. And so, we return to the idea that meditation can and should be an important part of education and, more particularly in the context of my overall argument, political education. Because (and this is my main theme) we need urgently to find ways of remedying the apparent inability of our political institutions to solve the grievous problems of current society.

This first chapter gives an overview of the argument as a whole. The second chapter explains in what sense "politics doesn't do what it says on the tin," and the third and fourth chapters explain and describe how meditation can help.

Politics and Emotion: 'Emotional Intelligence'

To begin with: neither politics nor meditation is ever simply a matter of 'applying the mind'. We need only to watch or listen to the uproar of a parliamentary debate to hear the intensity of the *emotions* in play – sometimes inspirational idealism but more often indignation, aggression and anger. And with respect to meditation, one of the most influential writers on the subject has suggested that effective meditational practice depends above all on managing to find *emotional equivalents* for our (conceptual, discursive) *thinking*[2].

To note the discrepancy between our thinking and our emotions, between our heads and our hearts, reminds us that although in certain respects the distinction is usually treated as obvious, the gap between the two is also often seen as highly regrettable, if not downright dangerous; and that finding a way of blending and integrating the two is an urgent necessity. This theme is summed up by the title of a book, 'Emotional Intelligence', by Daniel Goleman; and when it was published, in 1996, it immediately became, for the human sciences, a bestseller. What the book suggests is that because of a general lack of 'emotional intelligence' in the population, 'selfishness, violence and a meanness of spirit seem to be rotting the goodness of our communal lives.'[3] What Goleman proposes as a remedy is a redirection of educational policy in order to foster "essential human competencies such as empathy...compassion...self-awareness, self-control, and the arts of listening, resolving conflicts and co-operation"[4], i.e., *emotional intelligence*. As Goleman says, "The question is, how can we bring intelligence to our emotions – and civility and caring to our communal life." [5]

We may feel that it is difficult to disagree with any of this, but we might also then respond, 'Easier said than done'. The idea that we would all be better off if we could 'bring intelligence to our emotions' and thereby curb our selfishness and violence, and acquire instead such qualities as compassion and self-awareness, is obviously appealing; but we can immediately see that there is nothing really new about it. And this already alerts us to an obvious problem. The book was published in 1996 and the author, Daniel Goleman, writes, "I have had to wait till now before the scientific harvest [of research studies on the nature of emotion] was full enough to write this book." And yet, although it was immediately hailed as 'ground-breaking', in the quarter-century since it was published, our public affairs have seen no diminution whatsoever in the incidence of selfishness and violence. One thinks, for example of the unending warfare in the Middle East, the election of a whole series of self-serving and proudly xenophobic political leaders, the rising statistics concerning the involvement of young men in urban knife crime, and the report that in response to the outbreak of the coronavirus pandemic, the sale of guns in the United States reached a record level[6].

What this suggests, at the very least, is that the evidence of scientific research studies does not on its own cause us human beings to change our behaviour (even though some people seem to hope a pandemic might do so!). Perhaps, one might argue, a quarter of a century is not long enough for the message to sink in, i.e., for changes in educational aims and values to take effect. But even more telling than the lack of apparent progress in the time that has elapsed since the publication of *Emotional Intelligence* is the irony that Goleman begins his book by quoting Aristotle. In Book Four of his *Ethics,* Aristotle analyses the 'moral virtue' of what we might call 'intelligent' *anger* – one of the emotions that we might think of as being in particular need of regulation by our intelligence. For Aristotle the 'virtue' that brings intelligence to anger is *patience,* one of a number of qualities that are 'virtues' in the sense that they are characteristics that are generally agreed to be beneficial ('good') for *any* human being. The implications of this argument about 'virtues' will become important in the final section of Chapter Four. However, for the present the point is simply that if Goleman needs to cite Aristotle in support of his argument, it suggests that we have somehow managed to avoid putting into practice some widely available teachings on 'emotional intelligence' not just for a couple of decades but for nearly two-and-a-half thousand years. Which provokes the question: if this is such an important insight how and why have we failed, apparently, to act on it?

Anger, for Example...

Goleman presents Aristotle's analysis of anger as follows. It is "a rare skill to be angry with the right person, to the right degree, at the right time, for the right purpose and in the right way"[7]. Such carefully modulated anger is one of various 'moral virtues' that Aristotle examines, and Goleman's book is about the necessity that our *all* our emotions should be guided and channelled by a similarly careful intellectual and ethical awareness. Examples of other relevant emotions might be, for example, greed, envy and fear; but Aristotle's example of anger is important and instructive in considering general issues in both politics and meditation.

In some ways, political life is underpinned by anger; indeed, one might say that anger is implicitly designed into the central process of politics – of parliamentary democracies, at least. In simple terms, one political party is elected to govern, and the other parties have to be content with forming 'the opposition'. But governments are both fallible and partisan, and so the most important political role of the opposition is to seek out the inevitable shortcomings in government policies and to criticise them publicly as examples of injustice, self-interest, incompetence or disregard of ethical values. So, in this sense, although opposition parties do not of course have a monopoly of political anger, the public expression of anger could be described as the *central task* of an opposition in a properly functioning political system.

This is political anger in its minimal form, in the abstract, as it were. However, in practice the sources of political anger are both more varied and more intense, involving the whole spectrum of our emotions and even impulses to violent action. Indeed, and especially where the culture of competing political parties is not well established, election results are frequently contested as being invalidated by financial corruption or partisan violence; and the electoral process often leads directly to civil war. [8] Underlying all this is the basic fact that societies are made up of 'factions' based on ethnicity, religion, tribe, region or class, whose mutual distrust and hostility can all too easily be triggered. Consequently, a simple 'disagreement' over a policy or the choice of a candidate can easily set off expressions of general emotional antagonism.

And to cap it all, there is the question of power. The anger of a parliamentary opposition at the inadequacy of government policy may be intensified by its sense that the government's institutionally entrenched power means that it is impervious to the opposition's criticism. So, inevitably, rather than simply waiting for the next election, other arenas for the expression of political anger are opened up – strikes, protest marches, social media campaigns, civil disobedience. And the question always arises as to whether these extra-parliamentary expressions are effective as efforts to influence government policy. Supporters of the policies in question will usually say that the expressions of anger in these various campaigns are a danger to order, are perceived as objectionable by 'ordinary citizens', and are thus politically counterproductive. A further spiral of anger then frequently takes place when opposition groups blame the police and/or government-supporting media for claiming that the protests, strikes, etc. are indeed dangerous, objectionable and counterproductive. Thus, in the context of politics, anger can be seen as inescapable, endemic, and even perhaps as positive: [The flame of] "anger against injustice... [has] been burning...from the beginning of time in the hearts of everyone in every civilisation"[9].

But the question always arises as to how anger can be intelligently controlled in order to ensure that it is effective.

In meditation, the issue of anger arises very differently. In Buddhist meditation, for example, anger in the sense of general antagonism is one of the three universal poisons which render all human actions ineffective and usually even self-destructive. The preferred term for this poisoning element, however, is not 'anger' but 'hatred' or 'animosity', precisely because if anger is regulated by Aristotle's list of necessary judgements (the right person, to the right degree, at the right time, etc.), then anger can be righteous and 'skilful' – in Aristotle's terms 'virtuous', i.e., motivating us to be patient, vigorous and persistent in pursuit of what is ethical and just. And this clarifies the issue of the relationship between meditation and politics quite nicely. Because, unfortunately, a lot of political anger is much closer to animosity and hatred than to the Aristotelian, Buddhist or Golemanesque ideal of what we might call 'intelligent' anger: carefully timed, carefully directed, carefully expressed. Two questions arise, then: firstly, is this intelligent, 'righteous' anger just a theoretical possibility; and secondly, does meditation offer a practical method for subjecting our emotions (such as anger) to intellectual, strategic and, above all, ethical control? If so, we now need to clarify what sort of meditation we have in mind.

What Sort of 'Meditation'?

This is an important question because the 'politically helpful' form of meditation for which I am arguing needs to be differentiated clearly from other practices and other meanings of the term. Firstly, meditation has what might be called a *'common-sense'* meaning, which I have already referred to, namely 'applying one's mind' to thinking at length and carefully about an idea, a situation or a course of action; so that in a dictionary of synonyms we can find 'meditating' listed alongside, 'examining', 'pondering', 'reflecting', 'considering', etc. Clearly, things would be in a pretty chaotic state if we could not assume that this describes what politicians already engage in on a routine basis; and similarly, for those who try to influence them, and those who vote for them (i.e., ourselves). So, if this is all we mean by meditation my argument for the value of meditation would be difficult to refute but also rather superfluous!

Secondly, 'meditation' is used in many religious traditions to refer to a form of *devotional* practice. This can take the form of, for example, visualising the letters of the name of the Divinity or reciting sacred texts as mantras. In this sense, meditation is closely associated with prayer, and may even be a formal part of a ceremony of worship – in order to intensify a personal experience of Divine Love, a 'cosmic' awareness, or a sense of merging with a Supreme Being. These details are drawn from accounts of meditation in the Christian, Jewish, Hindu, and Islamic traditions, and many of them could also apply to some forms of Buddhism. But other forms of Buddhism, and other religious traditions, such as Quakerism, emphasise a less mystical form of meditation, where the focus is on experiencing with concentration and intensity aspects of our own human consciousness, rather than an external supernatural Being. Meditation in this sense becomes to some extent a matter of *self-understanding*. This is very much the emphasis in Buddhism (of which much more later); and Buddhist ideas and methods have had a direct influence on attitudes to meditation in other traditions, especially on Hinduism, with which Buddhism shares a lot of common history. But in any case, my argument is intended to be both ecumenical (embracing *any* faith) and secular. So, the form of meditation I am advocating is *not* devotional in either its purpose or its contents.

Thirdly, there is a well-known *medical-therapeutic* model of meditation used in the treatment of stress and depression. This is based on a form of 'mindfulness' derived from a secularised version of Buddhism, and involves an intense focusing of our attention in order to concentrate the mind fully on our experience in the present moment, without making any judgements or interpretations. In this way we can prevent our thoughts and emotions from dragging us into the unhelpful process of endless speculation and brooding, which so often perpetuates the symptoms of anxiety and depression.

'Mindfulness' is a key element in Buddhist teachings and Buddhist meditation practices, and the widely acknowledged success of this therapeutic application is an indication of the strength of what might be thought of as the secular, humanistic direction that Buddhism has taken recently, particularly in the West[10]. It is particularly helpful in that it indicates that the *'action'* of meditation involves 'directing our attention' towards a specific area or our experience. However, this is not just 'the present moment', helpful though this is as a starting point; rather, *any* area of our experience can become the focus for our attention. And so although the therapeutic, quasi-medical version of meditation, focussing on the treatment of depression and stress, is impressively successful[11], it rests on a rather narrower argument than the claim I wish to make for the relevance of Buddhist meditation in understanding political processes.

Meditation Practice and Buddhism

There is a very good reason why my main argument is based on *Buddhist* meditation, namely that the practice of meditation lies at the very heart of Buddhism. This is not the case for the other spiritual traditions mentioned earlier, where the foundation myth of the tradition focuses mainly on a divine Being as creator and judge, and the key practices involve prayer, cultural observances, and devotional ritual, with meditation as a sort of special option. In contrast, the foundation myth of Buddhism is, precisely, the story of a meditation. A young man leaves his home to seek a way of achieving a fuller and more reliable understanding of his experience. After finding the methods of two rather mystically oriented teachers to be unsatisfactory he finally remembers an episode from his youth – the pleasure of experiencing total concentration as he watches his father ploughing a field. He immediately recognises the importance of the insight contained in this youthful memory, and resolves he will sit and try to create a state of concentration like the one he remembers until he finds the form of understanding he seeks[12]. And he does. 'Awakening' from this, his first meditation, he is henceforth known as 'the Buddha', i.e., 'The Awakened One'.

What the Buddha 'awoke to' was a radically new approach to human experience. This consisted of new forms of understanding, each of which need to be acted up on in a certain way[13]. These new understandings focussed on the nature of suffering, the nature of lasting happiness (as opposed to the gratification of transient desires), and the basis for ethical behaviour. And this new understanding included a recognition that meditation itself is a central element in the path of discovery – for all of us, as it was for the Buddha.

In many ways The Buddha's teachings did not originally constitute a 'religion'. They did not, for example, emphasise accounts of a Divine creator or metaphysical speculation. Instead, they present a deep and wide-ranging examination of the basis of our experience – a sort of philosophical psychology – combined at every point with a focus on their practical ethical implications.

Ethical values – generosity, compassion, avoiding hatred or violence, etc – are always implicitly relevant in an obvious way for the conduct of political affairs. Indeed, The Buddha was frequently called upon to give advice to local rulers, and many of his teachings are quite explicitly concerned with the arrangements required in a just and well-governed society[14]. But although we may find accounts of the political importance of ethical values, derived from whatever tradition – religious or secular – to be interesting, intellectually convincing, and emotionally powerful, they do not necessarily make us change the way we act. They might, but there again, they might not!

In contrast, the forms of meditation for which I am arguing not only consist of ethical precepts or parables that are *intended* to help us change our views and our values, but also, and most importantly, forms of *practical action* that actually require us *to engage in changing* ourselves and our relationships. In other words, what is specific about Buddhist meditation is that its aim, from the outset, is not only to change our understanding but to change the way we habitually respond to events, to other people, and to our own feelings; and in this way to make our *actions* more considered, more reflective and more self-aware. Thus, the principle of *generosity* that is so central in Buddhist values is not so much a moral requirement but the 'natural' consequence of a sort of practical wisdom.

And this takes us straight back to Aristotle. Aristotle's analysis of 'virtuous' anger seems at first to have an obvious limitation How do I decide who is the 'right' person to be angry with in a situation until I have had time to analyse the contribution of everyone involved? How can I decide what is the 'right' degree of anger until I have already responded in a particular way and noticed whether or not it has been helpful – to me and to others? And ditto as regards the 'right' time, and so on? We may agree that Aristotle has identified the sort of knowledge we need in order to avoid being misled by impetuous emotional impulses to act in a way that is, from our own perspective, destructive. But it seems to be the sort of knowledge we only gain in retrospect, i.e., when it is too late to *guide our words and actions*, on this occasion, in this moment.

In contrast, what we really need in order to solve the 'problem' of our anger, is not merely 'knowledge' (an improved *analysis* of anger – important as that maybe) but a form of *practical understanding* that we can lodge deeply in our emotions, in our awareness of our experience, and in our responses. And our responses of course affect the way we behave, because they can become *habitual*; so that they can be relied upon to inform our responses to further situations as they occur.

From this perspective a similar issue is raised by Socrates' famous statement in his 'Apology', about the importance of *examining* the way we lead our lives: "The unexamined life is not worth living." 'Examining' sounds as though it aims at clarifying the *concepts* underpinning our knowledge rather than *awakening* the sort of emotionally grounded understanding and practical ways of acting that would inevitably lead us to change the way we lead our lives.

So, what do we mean when we say that Buddhist meditation is not just a matter of 'examining' but a form of 'awakening'? First of all, it involves a more than usually intense form of *awareness* – not only of our mental activity, but also of our feelings and our physical sensations; and also of the ethical implications of other people's responses to us and our responses to them. And this also involves *directing* our awareness towards a certain aspect of our experience at a particular moment. This in turn entails recognising that we have this capability – i.e., of directing and concentrating and thereby *integrating* our attention, which otherwise tends to be rather fragmented, as various thoughts and impulses 'occur' to us, one leading to another.

Secondly, we 'awaken' to a *sense of the need for change*. The first teaching that the Buddha gave after his own awakening was that there are ways (including meditation) in which we can understand and *ease* the 'suffering' that seems to be such an inescapable part of our lives. There is some dispute as to whether 'suffering' is the appropriate word here. Of course, for some people, in the midst of war, illness, poverty, starvation or bereavement, 'suffering' is exactly the right word. But for those of us who for the time being are less afflicted, there is still that near-universal sense that life is 'somehow not quite right.' This takes many forms: awareness that what we crave for is in the end transient or just disappointing; sorrow as we anticipate the ultimate loss of family and friends; an existential anxiety about our lives' lack of 'meaning'; a fear of death; a sense of our inadequacy, or remorse at the memory of moral failing. All of this can motivate a desire for some sort of change in the way we understand ourselves and our interactions with others, and a recognition of how both may be connected with the political processes within which we live.

But we awaken also to a sense of the need for political change on a larger scale, as suggested by the examples listed at the beginning of this chapter. In our current age of multimedia twenty-four-hour news coverage we cannot avoid an awareness of injustice, suffering, and extreme inequality on a local and a global scale, all of which seem to have been going on for as long as we can remember. And this can easily generate a sense of our inescapable complicity, leading to anxiety, frustration, anger, and grief.

However, and thirdly, as part of the meditation process we also awaken to a renewed confidence in the *possibility* of change – a renewed confidence in our own energies and a renewed understanding that all external situations and events are changing – and inevitably, necessarily so. So that what we *awaken from*, we might say, is also a sense of *despair* – because our politics just *isn't working,* is not 'doing what it says on the tin.' In other words, we awaken from the delusion that change is either unnecessary or impossible: we recollect that we can always make some sort of political contribution, even if it is only writing a letter of protest, joining a campaign or supporting a charity[15].

I noted earlier that the solution to a complex problem in our affairs is often said to be a change of 'culture'. And that this is never very helpful, because 'culture' is such an all-inclusive term that it immediately begs the question: OK – but when we look at all the different factors that might possibly be at work here, how do we decide where to start? And this is where meditation, as a 'solution', is different. Because describing meditation as an 'awakening' reminds us that meditation is a series of actions – a practical process, not a static state in which we contemplate a set of interesting possibilities. Buddhists always refer to meditation as a 'practice', as something we *do*. And this gives us a set of potentially effective starting points (as will be described in chapter three). And at the same time meditation is in its own way 'all-inclusive', in that it involves *all* aspects of our being – our concerns, our awareness and our aspirations.

Finally, and most importantly, meditation is not a 'one off' action. Rather it is a sustained effort which only 'works' if we manage to practise it in such a way that it becomes a regular habit. There is nothing strange or intimidating about this. We know that if we wish to make progress in a sport, or juggling, or in playing a musical instrument we need to 'practise' on a regular basis, and in the same way we need to 'practise meditation'. Put it another way: awareness, mindfulness and awakening are like rather under-used muscles; we need to tone them up and increase their strength by regular visits to the gym! Progress in meditation often seems a bit slow – as with any sort of training. But we don't need to be discouraged: the Buddha continued to meditate all his life, and according to the early texts he was a particular fan of breathing meditation[16], which is also where most of us start (see Chapter Three).

Chapter Two
Why Politics Doesn't Do
What It Says on the Tin

In this chapter I suggest what is 'wrong' with our politics; and in the following chapter how meditation might contribute to putting it right. My overall argument in this chapter is that politics 'doesn't do what it says on the tin' in the sense that key terms of political debate, i.e., terms that our politics proudly displays 'on its tin', so to speak, just 'don't work'. We all think that these terms identify in a straightforward and helpful way the central value of our political life, but they turn out to be awkwardly ambivalent in practice, misleading us instead into frustrating dilemmas and contradictions that we experience as distressing.

Thus, for several years, and long before the Covid-19 virus came to haunt us in 2020, the plaintive message that 'politics is broken' was repeated almost every day on the BBC and in British newspapers. The complaints tended to focus on the 'tone' of political debate – its anger, its ferocity, its rudeness. It was suggested that a previously existing consensus concerning underlying values, such as 'tolerance', 'community', 'freedom of expression' and mutual respect' had somehow been lost. But the shock administered by the virus suddenly expanded and deepened the message. On the one hand we heard *hope* expressed, that the 'external' threat of the pandemic would enable us, or even force us, to rediscover that lost consensus. On the other hand, there was the *fear* that we were not just facing a broken political system but a broken economy also, so that perhaps our social order was now broken in so many ways that we could hardly imagine what the 'repaired' consensus would look like.

In the pre-Covid-19 world, 'broken politics' seemed to be some sort of cultural malaise, expressing a sense of disappointment or dismay ('Surely, our politics *shouldn't be like this*'). Whereas the impact of the pandemic created a quite different set of problems that were presented as requiring the combined technical, scientific expertise of medicine, statistics, and economics. But inevitably, the science was politically disappointing. Doctors, virologists, statisticians and economists all had to acknowledge the unpredictability of individual cases and the multiplicity of factors involved; so that experts, unable to offer precise predictions, could only offer us a range of possibilities; and political policy statements were bemoaned as neither clear nor definite. And, even worse, there seemed also to be an inherent tension, which could not be ignored or disguised, between the predictions of the different forms of scientific expertise: what was required for economic growth was not the same as what was required for public health and safety. Even though it was claimed with equal frequency that a healthy citizenry needs a healthy economy, and vice versa.

Nevertheless, pandemic or no pandemic, in this chapter I shall not approach the question of what is wrong with politics by trying to diagnose it from a spiritual, ethical or political point of view as a 'malaise'. Nor shall I be presenting a critique claiming to be based on objective scientific evidence. (Statisticians deal in probabilities based on contestable data with unclear implications, medical evidence always depends on the uniqueness of the individual human organism, and economists are notoriously only able to predict the past.) Instead, I will analyse our experience of politics in terms of some underlying issues arising from and referring to something inherently paradoxical at the heart of our political processes and institutions. The terms identified as the focus for this chapter are 'consensus', 'trust', 'truth', and 'responsibility'.

After each issue has been explored there is a brief note indicating how some aspect of meditation practice could help us engage more effectively with the problems underlying these dilemmas and ambiguities. These references to meditation are illustrative indications only, and are cross-referenced to sections in the detailed descriptions of different meditation processes given in Chapter Three. It will gradually become clear that although the political issues are described separately, they are closely linked; and so of course there is also overlap between the various references to meditation.

The Problem of 'Consensus'

It is ironic that politicians and political journalists refer so frequently to 'consensus' in a tone of wistful longing, even nostalgia. Ironic because, as noted in the previous chapter, contemporary politics is usually supposed to be founded on the basis of *debate* between parties that are *competing* for office. The principle that the party of government can be voted out of office by an opposition with *different policies* is held to be the basis for all our freedoms, so much so that in many parts of the world the phrase 'one-party-state' is generally taken to be a synonym for oppressive dictatorship even when the material benefits achieved for the population are widely reported to be immense (e.g., China). In the case of a regime where a single political organisation successfully manages a process of mass participation in which decisions are actually arrived at by gradually negotiating a consensus rather than by establishing which side of a question is supported by majority [17] – it arouses surprisingly little interest.

On the other hand, it is also generally true that for a politician to be seen to have placed 'party advantage' above 'the national interest' is a particularly damaging accusation. Indeed, a critique of 'party politics' was a recurrent theme in the immensely popular American TV series *The West Wing*. Over seven years an idealised president (always courageous, patriotic, humorous, knowledgeable and humane) bemoaned the way in which ethically irreproachable policies had to be watered down, sullied and often defeated by the competing 'party machines' that dominate the law-making process. The series ran from 1999 to 2006. In 2016 the theme was even more controversially brought up to date in *Designated Survivor*, where the two political parties were seen to be tearing apart the governmental process, and it was left to a president who was officially an 'Independent' to gradually knit together a fabric of consensus and trust.

So, we have the interesting paradox that our political culture tends to proclaim two apparently incompatible ideals:

rigorous debate between competing political parties and, at the same time, 'cross-party' / 'bi-partisan' consensus. It seems as though we can't help longing for the sort of certainty that 'consensus' implies, even though we also recognise that complete certainty is an impossible dream. Perhaps it might seem to be quite straightforward to envisage consensus about general procedures while holding different opinions about specific policies. But of course, there could be disagreement as to which is which. For example, a given voting procedure could seem to give advantage to a group that is in favour of a particular policy.

Or perhaps we might not need competing parties at all, if the government's decisions were to be scrutinised by a regulatory body that is strong and independent enough to guarantee our freedoms. But this leads to the obvious question: who will regulate the regulators? (And then: who will regulate the regulators of the regulators? – an infinite regress, of course.) So, we are left with what seems to be an insoluble dilemma entangling two of our most cherished political ideas: consensus and freedom, both of which underpin our image of a safe and caring community.

A similar issue arises in relation to the question of 'party unity'. Party members causing 'disunity' are criticised for damaging the chances of the party's future electoral success, even though they always claim to be following their conscience and to be acting 'on principle'. Their supporters claim, of course, that we should admire a 'conscientious' politician more than one who merely 'toes the party line'.

Perhaps there really is an inevitable tension in political life between party-political pragmatism and individual conscience, but we might suggest that the problem also arises from certain deep-seated features of the organisations we create and inhabit. We know that in theory an organisation is a group of people and a series of carefully structured processes aiming to pursue, as efficiently as possible, a particular set of goals. This applies to a hospital, a car manufacturer and (equally) a political party. But we also know that in practice things are not so simple. We know from experience that within any organisation there will be individuals with differing ideas of what should be the focus of their energies. And over time these individuals are likely to join with others and to act together as a 'subgroup', in order to further their interests. In particular, senior executives may put a lot of effort into protecting their powerbase against subordinates. For example, senior Ministers in the UK government continue to make sure that ordinary members of parliament are prevented from directly interrogating government officials, since that would undermine ministers' own ability to control flows of information[18], even though a change in this policy would clearly result in greater access and transparency, which would be in the interests of the democratic process as a whole.

The disunity caused by the 'displacement' of organisational goals by the self-interested motives of a subgroup within the organisation is not limited to managers (although managers' behaviour in this respect was the first to be formally recognised as an issue[19]. On the contrary, 'goal displacement' is a more or less universal phenomenon, because there are as many potentially self-interested subgroups in an organisation as there are different roles. As regards the unity/disunity of political parties, the most general perspective is that any group that is conscious of itself *as* a group is quite likely to become just as concerned with maintaining itself as with the broader aims that are supposed to define the organisation's purpose. [20]

It is important not to oversimplify the problem. Our behaviour regularly has more than one 'goal' at a time; and so the problem of goal 'displacement' is usually more often a question of ambiguity rather than sheer hypocrisy. Thus, two or three subgroups within a political party may appear to have formed around alternative policy proposals (lower taxation or not; increased public expenditure or not), each claiming to be 'more in touch with the electorate' than the other. But at the same time, at another level, these different subgroups may also have coalesced around alternative prospective candidates for future leadership, and are thus as much concerned with individual career advantage as the proper policy direction for the party. All of which suggests once again how easily disunity arises in our affairs, reminding us that 'consensus' may be more of an ever-receding vision than a practical aspiration.

But perhaps to understand this paradox we need to dig even deeper. Perhaps the tendency for consensus to elude us is rooted in our evolutionary prehistory. For two-and-a-half *million* years human beings lived as small nomadic tribes numbering a few dozen or perhaps a few hundred, living (quite satisfactorily) on what we could forage. And it is only for ten *thousand* years that we have organised our lives in settled societies, based on agriculture and industrial manufacture, consisting of at first thousand and latterly millions of people [21].

This relatively recent and rapid transition means that we all suffer from what Harari calls 'memory overload'[22]. Our minds are well adapted to storing what we need to know about the relatively few people we meet face-to-face on a regular basis – we have had two-and-a-half million years' practice at this. But what we need to know about the workings of the rest of society depends on forms of knowledge that remain (after a mere ten thousand years) much more difficult for us because they just don't come naturally – writing, conceptual analysis, logic, and mathematics – i.e., the forms of knowledge that determine our lives in modern bureaucratic organisations, such as political parties and governments. What this means is that the problem we all need to address, and what would improve the quality of our organisational life, is not so much our 'memory overload' but what I should prefer to call our '*empathy* overload'.

Most of us can empathise with family members, friends, and people we know, people with whom we share opinions and values – our 'tribe'. But politics and political organisations require understanding on a much larger scale. Instead of which they are threatened by what is indeed often called political 'tribalism'. Larger political parties can sometimes defend themselves by making a virtue of being 'a broad church'; but the danger of 'sectarianism' is always present, as members find that they just can't cope with the irremediable difference of other people's points of view. The problem is beautifully satirised in the Monty Python film *The Life of Brian*, where members of 'The People's Front of Judea' are incensed at being taken for 'The Judean People's Front' and point derisively at the single member of 'The Popular Front of Judea' sitting in self-righteous isolation.

Meditation, in contrast, might help us to see the notion of political consensus in terms of an emotional craving that we can learn to let go; and our identification with our own 'tribal' subgroup as a form of egotism and a failure of imagination – see Chapter Three, sections iii and vi.

The Problem of 'Trust'

By a considerable margin, according to a survey published by *Forbes Magazine* in 2019, citizens of the United States trust their Members of Congress *less* than the members of any other profession, contrasting sharply with the perceived trustworthiness of nurses, doctors and pharmacists[23]. As a cultural phenomenon this is neither recent nor exclusive to the United States. When Onora O'Neill was invited to give the BBC Reith Lectures on the theme of 'Trust' twenty years ago in the UK, she began with the questions, "Is it true that we have stopped trusting? ... Is trust obsolete/"[24]. This is, of course, a very worrying problem: long before 2002 (in the sixth century BC to be exact) Confucius advised that trust is the most important basis for government, more important even than food, because "Death has always been with us since the beginning of time, but when there is no trust, the common people will have nothing to stand on" [25].

So here is another paradox in our political life: we go through an elaborate process of choosing people to govern us, and thereby give them the authority to make key decisions that may affect our lives quite dramatically. And yet we don't trust them. How can this be?

One approach to this issue is through the notion of 'representation'. Members of a government are almost always elected as 'representatives', not as 'delegates'. This means that although they are elected on the basis of a set of policies published as a manifesto, during the interval between elections we must trust them to make their own decisions as to how the manifesto is to be interpreted in response to different historical situations as they arise. If, in contrast, they were 'delegates' we could insist on being consulted afresh as situations changed, so that we could 'recall' a member of parliament whose decisions we disagree with (if, for example, we feel that they have broken an election promise). So, we might say that 'delegates' are elected *provisionally*, subject to recall if a majority of their electorate so desire. Whereas the election of representatives requires us to trust those we have elected to act according to our wishes faithfully and accurately *in situations we have not yet envisaged.* We can immediately see that such an arrangement is in principle beset with problems; and yet if we try to solve the problems by insisting on a universal 'right of recall' many would argue that it would result in an endless and unwieldy series of referendums.

What might make this dilemma tolerable would be the confidence that we can trust our political representatives because they are 'like us': i.e., at a deep level they share our opinions, our view of the world, our values. While this clarifies the problem, it does not solve it. In large-scale societies electorates always consist of a variety of *different* cultures, so that individual elected representatives, no matter how well-meaning and sociable, are bound to leave some of their electorate feeling excluded in some respect or other. There is also an ever-present tendency to feel that elected politicians create their own culture – what critics like to call 'The Bubble'. The term refers to the legislative institutions, with their esoteric, inward-looking procedural rules and rituals, competing always for electoral advantage, systemically serving 'The Establishment' and ignoring the concerns of 'us the people'. This then creates the political space in which 'populist' politicians can rise to power, claiming they alone can be trusted because they represent 'the people' *against* The Establishment.

Another aspect of the problem is that the greater the level of inequality in a society the greater the problem of trust. A recent study reported that in Japan, Norway, Sweden and Finland, for example there are high levels of trust and low levels of inequality, whereas in Portugal and Singapore there are low levels of trust and high levels of inequality [26]. We can easily see why this might be so. If we perceive that the politicians who claim to represent us are aligned socially and culturally with those who are much wealthier than ourselves, we may be tempted to distrust them because we assume they will not fully sympathise with our problems. Whereas if we perceive them to be aligned with those who, compared to ourselves, are in poverty, some of us will distrust them because we will fear that, whatever the politicians say, they will probably have an agenda of redistributing resources to our disadvantage – reducing welfare spending and raising our taxes. And given that the rate of inequality is *in fact increasing* [27], these are particularly uncomfortable lines of thought, pointing to political motives and attitudes we would prefer to ignore. For example: on the one hand, envy; and on the other hand, disdain. These are rather embarrassing motives, of course, which is why politicians and journalists more frequently choose to blame low levels of trust on cultural differences, or on the legislative Bubble, or on the remoteness of The Establishment.

One way out of the problems concerning how far we are right to trust our political representatives was suggested long ago by Rousseau in *The Social Contract*, namely drawing lots; so that citizens would be appointed to a role in the government on a random basis, as was the case in ancient Athens (always excluding slaves and women of course!) and in the same way as we are currently appointed to be members of a jury. This at the very least would have the advantage that juries are generally more trusted than politicians:

"Public attitude surveys have shown continuing strong support for the jury system, trust that a jury would come to the right decision, and a belief that a criminal trial by jury is fairer than such a trial by a judge." [28]

Rousseau explains why, in principle, it is more 'democratic' to select a politician by drawing lots rather than by voting. Firstly, it means that the process 'gives every citizen a reasonable hope of serving his country'; and secondly, it means that holding a public office is 'not a benefit' (with all the attendant risks of corruption that we see reported everyday) but 'an onerous duty', and therefore likely to attract only those who are motivated by a sense of public service rather than by self-interest [29]. And after long being ignored, Rousseau's radical suggestions have recently begun to attract attention and advocates. Intriguing experiments with innovative forms of representation, including 'sortition' (i.e., drawing lots), have taken place in Canada, The Netherlands, Iceland and Ireland [30].

Rousseau's general argument about filling governmental roles by drawing lots culminates in his declaration of 'trust' in 'the common sense, equity and integrity' of 'all citizens', reminding us that problems of trust can be re-phrased as problems of what we might call 'faith'. If we don't have faith in our citizens, our politicians and our political institutions, what do we have faith in? Where are we prepared to place our trust? What do we 'have confidence in'? What do we 'believe in' (in our everyday lives, rather than theologically)? At this everyday level we have already noted one popular answer: medicine, and more generally 'science' – above all the mythical science that 'delivers certainty'. As I write, at the height of the Covid-19 emergency in 2020–21, political discourse is indeed turning increasingly to medical science. News bulletins focus unendingly on the latest statistics (of infections, 'side-effects', hospitalisations, etc.) even though most of us are at a loss to understand their implications for our experience.

But under normal circumstances the scientific version of political affairs usually comes under the heading of economics. So, do we trust the science of economics? For many years, since Bill Clinton won the 1992 USA presidential election with the slogan, 'It's the economy, stupid', the answer to this question was, 'Yes, of course'. Since then, trust in economics as a science took a tumble when almost all economists failed to predict the system-wide collapse of financial institutions in 2008 (mainly because their own ingenuity created products that were so opaque that they did not know how to trust each other). But what did seem to survive intact as an object of faith and trust was that lynchpin of classical economic theory – The Market. And we can understand why. The value of The Market to politicians and political commentators is that its operations can be presented in terms of numerical evidence, and so the decisions arising from predicting the operation of The Market can be presented as apparently nonpartisan, objective and non-controversial.

However, the basis for our continuing trust in this line of argument is by no means clear. For example, it remains politically controversial, in spite of all the various market-based arguments, that government debt must *necessarily* involve reductions in the provision of social security and education; that in order to be profitable, manufacturing *must* be switched from Europe to *low-wage economies* in southeast Asia; that delivery drivers *do not need* holiday – or sick-pay; that care-home workers, being *unskilled*, should be paid no more than *the minimum wage*; that trees in the Amazon rain forest should be chopped down to make way for *more profitable* land-use in order to increase the rate of growth of the Brazilian economy; or that the highest paid CEOs, because of their enormous value to their companies, should receive 386 times the income of a worker on the UK 'national living wage' [31].

So, what is it that leads us to trust in the workings of The Market, even though their outcomes, judging by the examples listed above, are quite generally agreed to be controversial and, in some quarters, objectionable? An answer begins to emerge as soon as we consider the ambiguities in the legacy of Adam Smith, icon and honorary founder of market theory. The Adam Smith Institute, founded in 1977 and with a dominant influence in political thinking ever since, not only propagates Smith's ideas but also proclaims itself as being 'at the forefront of making the case for free markets and a free society…and using free markets to end poverty' [32].

'Free society' and 'ending poverty' sound good, but how are they supposed to come about? Adam Smith's most famous quotation, found in any student's basic textbook of economics, is: 'Every individual…neither intends to promote the public interest…he intends only his own gain, and he is in this, as in many other cases, led by an invisible hand to promote an end which was no part of his intention.' [33] This is interpreted by the economics establishment as meaning that 'the market' creates economic justice as a natural outcome of equilibrium between self-interested buyers and self-interested sellers. Decision-making can thus be analysed technically and mathematically, based on an assumption of universal rational self-interest, without recourse to the variety of individual motivation, to ethical values, or political policy preferences. In order to create 'a free society' and to 'end poverty', all we need to understand is 'the general equilibrium of supply and demand.' [34]

Well, we know that is how most economists think, and of course we feel its attraction: it promises to satisfy, by means of mathematical modelling, exactly that desire for certainty and consensus described in the previous section. But we have also learned to be sceptical: we recognise that its implicit optimism (ending poverty simply by means of a free market) rests on a strange simplification of human action, ignoring and even denying the complexity of our motives, our idiosyncrasies and our ethical being. We are increasingly aware, for example, that the economics of the free market leads to the indiscriminate pursuit of economic growth and (consequently) the systematic destruction of the planet. We know that politicians have known of this for decades and we wonder why they have not been able to prevent it happening.

And we know that these decades of 'free markets' have by no means 'ended poverty' but on the contrary led to extraordinary and continuing discrepancies between poverty and wealth [35].

Our mistrust of politicians' and economists' recourse to The Market to justify their decisions seems all the more justified when we examine Adam Smith's own thinking. Smith intended his work on economics to be part of an overall philosophical treatise that he had begun with his book *The Theory of Moral Sentiments.* The opening words of the first chapter ('Of Sympathy') are the exact *opposite* of a statement of belief that we can safely entrust our collective well-being to market operations based on self-interest:

'How selfish soever man may be supposed, there are evidently some principles in his nature, which interest him in the fortune of others, and render their happiness necessary to him, though he derives nothing from it except the pleasure of seeing it. Of this kind is pity or compassion.'[36]

Moreover, Smith's own accounts of economic relations, in *The Wealth of Nations,* do not always display the dispassionate stance of a 'scientific' economist but quite often both compassion and anger. For example, he paints a moving picture of the unequal struggle over wages between masters and workmen – the masters able quite easily to combine together, while the law prohibits a similar combination of workers; and the workers in the end starved into submission. He suggests that wherever members of a trade association meet together, there is always the likelihood of 'a conspiracy against the public', and is particularly scathing about the role of financiers ('dealers'): they are 'an order of men...who have generally an interest to deceive and even to oppress the public, and who accordingly have upon many occasions, both deceived and oppressed it' [37].

We are not surprised, therefore, to discover that Adam Smith's optimistic belief that an 'invisible hand' will resolve our conflicts of interest does *not* spring from assumptions concerning the objectivity of mathematical models of market operations. Rather, the 'invisible hand' is that of 'Providence' [38], or in other words: 'that divine Being, whose benevolence and wisdom have, from all eternity, contrived and conducted the immense machine of the universe, so as at all times to produce the greatest possible quantity of happiness' [39]. This was conventional thinking when Smith was writing, in the eighteenth century, but probably, for most of us, not a part of our own beliefs. Either way, we can invoke Adam Smith's venerable authority in *mistrusting* politicians (no matter how confident) when they seem to be suggesting that 'The Economy, Stupid!' can provide us with an ethical and emotional get-out clause. And Adam Smith himself would surely encourage us to mistrust a version of politics that seems to suggest that our response to public issues concerning 'the wealth of nations' can be separated from our private 'moral sentiments'.

Meditation is unambiguous in encouraging us to <u>question</u> some of our impulses both of trust and of mistrust; and, in particular, to feel uncomfortable about accepting self-interest as the basis for the conduct of our affairs – see Chapter Three, sections iv and v.

The Problem of 'Truth'

"Why do you lie all the time? Wouldn't it be better if you just told us the truth?" The question was put to a panel of politicians in the BBC TV programme 'Question Time' [40]. Why indeed? We can all sympathise. In everyday life and in general, telling 'the truth' is supposed to be the basis of all social existence: a syndicate of fraudsters needs to assume that its members are telling each other the truth; otherwise, they could never plan or co-ordinate their criminal operations.

Where politics is concerned, however, as regards truth-telling, there is at best ambiguity. Although political leaders in several countries currently (2021) face accusations of large-scale corrupt financial dealings – Israel, France, and Brazil spring immediately to mind – the principle of 'transparency' is often invoked; both as a claim ('we have always made it absolutely clear that...') and as a demand ('will the Minister please explain exactly what happened when...'). But in practice, politicians seem more often to be seeking *plausibility* rather than truthfulness. In other words, in the world of politics, the important question is not so much, "Is this true?" but "Who will be persuaded by this?" Thus, an item of news is quite likely to be presented by a political commentator as a 'narrative'; and whereas we assume that there is only one truth for us to uncover, we can readily accept that there are always a number of different narratives competing for 'persuasiveness', i.e., plausibility. Thus, political commentators invite us to speculate, when a new political policy initiative is announced, whether the 'dominant' (i.e., more persuasive) narrative is going to be the implications of the policy for citizens or the threat to the leadership posed by those who disagree with it. We are then impelled to ask, who is 'orchestrating' or 'choreographing' these narratives, and why – with what motives and resources? New narratives are also made more appealing by linking them with favourite themes from the past, such as victories or dangerous enemies, and with clearly identifiable contemporary heroes or villains.

Governments in power claim to have a special relationship with Truth, because they have a responsibility to preserve the stability of current institutions, leading to issues of security. In the UK opposition politicians and investigative journalists seeking to uncover the truth about a murky set of events can make an application under the Freedom of Information Act. However, when the relevant documents are published much of it is sometimes blacked out in order to 'protect the innocent', whose security (we are told) would otherwise be endangered. We can appreciate this; and yet we also can't help worrying about the very unclear dividing line between protecting the innocent and protecting the government from the revelation of an unwelcome narrative or inconvenient evidence. For example, we can easily remember cases where 'whistle-blowers' following their own consciences and acting in accordance with the highest humanitarian principles have revealed the disturbing contents of government documents (courageously, we thought), and have then been accused of breaches of security amounting to treason.

No wonder we, the electorate, feel frustrated and confused. In our day-to-day lives to be caught out telling a lie is a cause for major embarrassment. But in politics, 'Truth' itself is a contested concept. At one extreme, the symptoms are almost comic: political leaders feel able to announce their achievements in terms that cannot possibly have a factual basis: Donald Trump congratulated his own unilateral agreement with the Israeli government as the "the deal of the century", and Boris Johnson repeatedly claimed that his repeatedly late and inadequate testing arrangements for the Covid-19 virus was "a world-beating system". But such examples are not just the eccentricities of individuals. Government policies will always be open to challenge, and so, when accused by journalists or opposition politicians of incompetence, lack of foresight or injustice, those speaking on behalf of the government will naturally start by putting a rosy gloss on their achievements. They will then take refuge in ignoring, evading, or misrepresenting any challenging questions put to them. For example, the question, "Will you apologise for this mistake, which has caused such widespread suffering and injustice?" might be answered by something like "Of course, I am extremely sorry if people feel upset..."

At another level, the issue of truth is even more obviously contaminated. Leading politicians are quite prepared to dismiss any investigations detrimental to their interests, ideology or reputation as 'Fake News' or 'a witch-hunt'. The validity of such accusations is plausible ultimately because we know that news corporations represent enormously powerful financial and political interests. Consequently, the owners and managers of newspapers, TV companies and social media platforms feel that they cannot afford to report in detail anything tending to undermine the interests of the social, political and financial Establishment on which the prosperity of the company depends; and this is likely in the end to outweigh concern for balanced coverage of contentious issues.

The problem of the link between 'truth' and political power is seen with particular clarity when we consider the foreign policy initiatives called 'covert operations'. The principle at work here is officially termed *plausible deniability*, i.e., management of political affairs so that senior staff can 'plausibly disclaim responsibility' [41], precisely because they actually *are* responsible. So, although *'transparency'* is said to be one of the key values on which effective political communication depends, the widespread existence of 'covert operations' reminds us that *concealment* is a regular feature of political affairs.

Not only is the role of systematic deception in political life currently and increasingly a matter of concern; concealment in political discourse has a long history. In the words of Machiavelli, writing in 1513:

'[The ruler] should *appear* to be compassionate, faithful to his word, kind, guileless, and devout... If he has these qualities and always behaves accordingly, he will find them harmful; if he only *appears* to have them, they will render him service.' [42]

Is anyone really surprised, by this, or even shocked? Or have we come to accept that the necessary skills of a successful politician will probably include persuasive deception – sometimes 'for the greater good' but sometimes out of naked self-interest? And can we easily tell which is which?

This question lies at the heart of many of our most popular films and TV series. Night after night we see fictional characters possessing wealth and power ('fictional' yes but also highly reminiscent of familiar public figures) engaged in conspiracy and corruption. The corruption is elaborately and ingeniously concealed, so how, we wonder, following the hero (police officer or journalist or lawyer) as the plot unfolds, is Conspiracy going to be exposed and Truth (the moral order of the community) reasserted? So here again there is an interesting paradox: one of our most familiar cultural themes, and an endless source of our entertainment, is the inescapable *problem of truth* in our social and political affairs: on the one hand, its absolute necessity as an ethical principle, contrasted with its continual absence in practice. As entertainment the issue is one which we can *enjoy*, secure in the knowledge that – in the end and to some extent – the 'mystery' will always be solved and the 'truth' will, somehow, emerge. But the implication is that such fictions are so ubiquitous precisely because so many of us believe that deception and corruption are endemic in our institutions, as part of the political reality we inhabit.

Is this 'just entertainment'? Or should we be seriously worried? Because we are so dependent, in all areas of life, on truth-telling as the foundation of our communication with one another, it is difficult to know whether or not we are exaggerating the scope of the problem. Admittedly, the rapid spread of 'Fake News', threatens us all with a sense that our attempts to understand events are doomed to failure. But the phrase 'speaking truth to power' has retained some of its moral and intellectual authority: it was first used as the title of a Quaker peace pamphlet in the 1950s [43], and only today (2020) I see it included as the key phrase in a newspaper obituary celebrating a life of courage and authenticity: 'He always spoke truth to power'. However, we may think that the eminent political critic Noam Chomsky was probably right when he quipped, 'Power already knows the truth, and is busy denying it' [44].

In meditation, however, we practise 'directing our attention' in such a way that we come adept in spotting and discounting delusion and self-deception on the part of our leaders, our opponents and, of course, ourselves. And the 'truth' we pursue is inseparable from compassion – see Chapter Three, sections iii and v...

'Responsibility'

The nature and origins of our responsibilities, as individuals and as members of a social and political community are issues that rightly cause us serious concern and even anxiety. Even the etymology of the word 'responsibility' is suggestive. Who are we 'answerable' to? What sort of questions must we be prepared to give a 'response 'to? And indeed, who will interrogate us? These questions and anxieties go back a long way. To the beginning of The Biblical Old Testament at least, where Cain, asked about the whereabouts of his younger brother replies: "Am I my brother's keeper?"[45] Even though this is usually seen as inexcusable flippancy, it does raise interesting issues about the *scope* of our responsibilities, Firstly, are my responsibilities for others to be carefully circumscribed (and by whom), or do my responsibilities include the whole of another's well-being – as his or her 'keeper'? Secondly, should Cain, as the elder, be considered the 'responsible' brother? And thirdly, who is 'my brother' – just a single family member, or perhaps all human beings? So, what light does Cain's response to the Lord's interrogation throw on the problems and paradoxes surrounding our feelings about the responsibilities of politicians?

First, we cannot escape a deep disappointment when we type 'responsible government' into our website browser and see that these large and interesting issues are sidestepped by defining the 'responsibility' of governments as merely matters of procedure. The website simply refers us to the ancient principle that the executive branch of the government is 'responsible' (answerable) to a house of elected members of parliament. This means that government ministers must 'make statements' in parliament concerning the affairs of their department, so that they can 'answer questions' put by members. And if there is a contentious issue, the relevant minister can be *summoned* to make a statement and answer questions [46]. Although this is presented as the very essence of parliamentary democracy, and although sometimes the shouting and applauding looks and sounds quite dramatic, much of the process is highly conventionalised. From this point of view, what ought to be a crucial aspect of our politics is mere spectacle, which on the one hand we can enjoy, but which we are also implicitly invited to take for granted.

So let us instead return to take seriously Cain's question about the *scope* of his responsibility for his brother. With respect to the scope of governmental responsibilities, the most immediate and familiar issue is that of timescale, which arises from the constitutionally limited term of an elected parliament. Because of this crucial element in the political process the government in power is always tempted to focus on one simple short-term pragmatic consideration: on the date of the next election, when the results of any given policy have got to be defensible, 'look good' and 'appeal to the electorate'. In other words, the implicit primary political responsibility becomes winning the next election and thereby preserving the careers of members of the party and the government.

In contrast, of course, the effects of the political policies that most concern us become apparent only after a much longer period than the interval between elections: policies concerning investment in airports, railways, social services and education, and attempts to reduce environmental degradation. The potential conflict between the two timescales – the short-term self-interest of the ruling party seeking re-election contrasted with the long-term wider interests for which we think a democratic government should be 'answerable' – becomes more acute as the date of the next election approaches. So, what is the timescale that a government should have in mind when it is taking seriously its responsibilities beyond immediate electoral advantage? The lifetime of the nation's children, maybe, or the nation's grandchildren or even the nation's great-grandchildren? There is heated debate along these lines, but on what possible basis could we try to decide?

This seems like an impasse; however, there is a way forward. A more comprehensive perspective on the timescale issue is nicely summed up in the notion of 'stewardship'. Human beings are mortal; and so we need to engage with all aspects of our lives as though we were 'stewards', i.e., as temporary managers or tenants, rather than as permanently entitled property-owners – and this applies to governments as well as individuals. The religious implications of stewardship are quite familiar. We human beings have been temporarily entrusted with this world by a Divine Creator, and are thus 'answerable' both to The Creator and also to future generations (who will themselves also be part of 'Creation') to hand it on in what we might call 'good working order'.

But when we start to argue along these lines, we are clearly not only thinking just about our great-grandchildren but about the planet that they will have to live on. We see that our responsibilities include issues like the preservation of biodiversity, global warming as a result of fossil fuel policies, and the pollution of the oceans with plastics. With this added dimension, the argument about responsibility has a sufficient backing of physical evidence, scientific theory and ethical principle to enable us to insist that our politicians make judgments about the proper scope of their responsibilities towards these 'wider interests' referred to above.

However, there is a further crucial aspect to the problem. Cain's question about the scope of his responsibilities is not about appropriate timescales. It is more of a question about who and what we are responsible *for*? If I am 'my brother's keeper', my responsibility is to *care for* him, to look after him, to make sure that he comes to no harm. And this is where the notion of *governmental* responsibility becomes controversial.

Some would say that a government goes beyond its responsibilities when it tries to 'look after' its citizens. In a democracy, it is argued, governments should simply manage the public finances with 'prudence' (encouraging 'growth' and avoiding 'waste'), so that citizens can 'exercise responsibility' in looking after themselves. So, for example, citizens should generously be given the facilities they need to set up a new enterprise, and citizens claiming public funds should meet with an official response that is tough, sceptical and appropriately wary of potential 'scrounging'. Indeed, as conventional economic theory would have it: 'well-meaning' governments that see it as their responsibility to 'care for' the well-being of its citizens more directly than this are always ill-advised and usually doomed to 'folly' [47]. The common phrase summing up this line of argument warns us against the dangers of the 'Nanny State'.

But 'Nanny State' is a strange term of abuse, we might think, especially now that the massive health scare of the Covid pandemic has alerted us to society's urgent need for 'care-workers'. Indeed, a 'Caring State', in contrast, we might argue, should see its responsibilities in the broadest possible terms: to counteract forms of institutionalised injustice, and to look after and defend rights and facilities for *all* citizens, and especially including the vulnerable; e.g., rights to legal aid, to medical treatment, to nursery and university education, and facilities for the protection for women, for the impoverished and for the homeless.

From this perspective, our first reply to Cain's question would be that we are indeed responsible for the well-being of our brother, and indeed for all our 'brothers'. Our sense that we exist as individual beings entirely separate from each other can be seen as a superficial illusion. Or, more poetically: 'I am a piece of the continent, a part of the main…any man's death diminishes me, because I am involved in mankind' [48]. This makes *empathy* a central principle in any serious consideration of our responsibilities, and also *imagination.* Both entail seriously trying to understand our fellow citizens, and this may well involve expanding our knowledge about the circumstances in which they live. Given the polarisation of material conditions in contemporary societies, it is easy to underestimate our responsibilities to others simply because we are so ignorant of how dramatically their lives differ from our own. As a very simple example, in one illuminating survey a group of wealthy bankers was asked to estimate the typical income of a family in '*poverty*'; but the figure they gave was in fact the same as the national *average income* [49].

Often, we simply do not know what it is that we do not know. The interconnectedness of events and the complexity of their causation make it difficult to know what we should be held accountable *for* and to whom we should be accountable. And at the same time the limitations of our knowledge make it almost impossible to have confidence in any hard-and-fast judgements as to how we and our politicians should formulate and carry out our responsibilities. We (the electorate) and the governments we elect are therefore always tempted to take the easy way out, to *limit* what we are willing to consider as our responsibilities to what does not disturb too much our self-interest. In this section I have tried to suggest why, although this is so obviously dangerous, we find it difficult to resist the temptation.

Meditation, on the other hand, reminds us of our interconnectedness with others, the impermanence of our possessions and relationships, and in this way always helps us imagine the potential scope of our responsibilities – see Chapter Three, sections i, v, and vi.

****

Taken together, the problems underlying the way we understand and practise 'consensus', 'trust', 'truth', and 'responsibility' make up a fairly broad view of our political worries and frustrations. *Frustrations,* because each term seems in itself to offer something like a helpful, straightforward principle; and *worries,* because, somehow, (whether as politicians or as citizens) we don't seem to be able to find a straightforward way of *acting* on these principles. Impressive political rhetoric we have in abundance; but satisfactory political action, not so much!

It could well be argued that there is nothing altogether new in this analysis, and some might well feel that a description of what is wrong with our politics could have focussed on a quite different set of terms – 'freedom', 'power', or 'democracy' for example. At the very least, they might argue, these terms should have been included. This is quite true, and indeed the foregoing arguments are not put forward as either original or comprehensive. Rather, I would like to suggest, they are just a way of indicating a sort of psychological and ethical 'space' in our political institutions and in our own political awareness, where, through meditation, we can (and need to) practise, precisely and intensively, a different set of responses.

Even the content of the meditation responses, as indicated above, will probably not seem surprising, but what really *is* new is the formulation of the meditation processes as forms of *'action'.* Delicate and subtle forms of action, of course: I'm talking about actions of the mind, heart and breath here, rather than throwing eggs at a policeman. But action, nonetheless, as opposed to merely 'thinking'. I indicated the nature of this distinction at the end of Chapter One, and it is intended to be implicit in the brief examples of meditation practices presented at the end of the various sections of this chapter. The distinction between thinking and meditation practice is one of the central arguments of the book as a whole, and it is the organising principle of the next chapter.

Chapter Three
Meditation – 'Be the Change...'

The teachings of religious traditions, those of Buddhism included, almost always include a set of moral values, such as love, generosity, truthfulness, sensitivity, responsibility, etc; and these readily form the starting point for critiques of contemporary economics and politics, focusing on issues such as injustice, inequality, consumerism, greed, planetary degradation, etc. [50]. However, although such critiques are valid and important in themselves, the analysis of meditation in this chapter uses Buddhist teachings in a different way and for a different purpose. It starts out from that wonderfully concise piece of advice usually attributed to Ghandi – but supposedly traceable originally to a car bumper sticker! [51] – 'Be the change you want to see in the world'

As advice this is excellent of course, and neatly focuses some very significant personal and political issues. After all, the message of Ghandi's advice has become familiar precisely because we understand its importance, even if we may sometimes forget it, or because we are not sure how to act on it. However, it begs the further question: how? How do we "be the change"? Or, disentangling the grammar: how do we change ourselves? And more precisely, how do we change our *habits*? Not *all* our habits, of course, just the ones that are unhelpful, those that seem to create depressing states of mind, humiliating interactions and counterproductive political responses – habits, in other words, that seem to be 'holding us back' and preventing us from playing our part in making the world a better place. Moreover, even supposing that we succeed in introducing much needed radical changes, we will need to promote and establish the 'new consciousness' that will be required to sustain these changes [52].

The meditation practices described in this chapter are all based on the distinction made in Chapter One between 'thinking about something' and forms of what we might call mental and emotional 'action', in which we *direct* our awareness in a specific direction, to focus on a particular object. Thus, each of the following sections describes a particular dimension or component of this 'meditation action process', indicating how, starting from one or more elements in the Buddhist teachings, it can form a starting point for a process of gradual *change* in our habitual responses. This chapter gives an *explanation* of meditation, rather than *'how to'* instructions on the various methods. These are presented later, in the 'Practical Guide to Meditation Methods'.

The Breath

We know that when we are on the point of doing or saying something ill-advised it is a good idea to 'take a deep breath'. The idea behind this is that we make mistakes when we are not concentrating, and that breathing provides the focus that we have temporarily lost. Or perhaps not so temporarily;

because so much of our experience is founded on thinking that is scattered, fragmented and blown hither and thither by apparently random connections in our brains; so that although we may feel quite focussed for short periods our thoughts seem continually to veer from one scenario to another. And where we end up is very much a matter of chance. This can be unpleasant and frustrating or (sometimes) creative, yielding unexpected 'good ideas'. But in either case quite different from the consciously focused experience of meditation.

When we meditate on the breath we introduce an effort of *concentration* into the act of breathing, and in this simple way we focus and *integrate* our thoughts, so that they are no longer so scattered, and inconsequential. The effect is not that our thinking suddenly becomes precisely purposeful, but that it attains a degree of *focussed awareness* (see section iii, below) as we begin to free ourselves from the normal pressures (sometimes casual, sometimes intense) of our everyday responses and interactions.

There is a longstanding tradition in breathing meditation that at first, we support our concentration by counting each breath [53], so that when we notice that we have lost count, we realise also that we have lost our concentration on the meditation practice. We also intensify our awareness of the breathing by 'watching' the breath on its journey from our nostrils and lips down to our lungs and back again. If we lose our concentration on the breath, because of an intrusive and unhelpful thought, we gently bring our attention back to the breath, from wherever it had ended up, carefully avoiding any sense of failure or self-blame.

Concentrated breathing has been a form of meditation from the very beginning of the Buddhist tradition, i.e., for about 2500 years. It is not difficult to see why this should be.

As a focus for concentrated awareness the breath has unique advantages: it is always *there,* it is crucially important, in that it keeps us alive (in Latin the word for breath is the same as the word for 'spirit', 'essence' or 'soul'), and it is also very *interesting.* For example, we can observe how the breaths vary in length; we can decide how much or how little we wish to control the breaths; and we can experience their deeply satisfying 'in-and-out' rhythm. And we can remember that we *share* the earth's atmosphere with all other breathing beings, including the trees that 'breathe out' the oxygen that we as human beings need to breathe in. This can lead to a feeling of *connectedness* with other creatures, helpfully undermining the implicitly egotistical self-centredness in our perception of ourselves as fundamentally separate beings...

One of the very earliest texts is a meditation practice whose title could be translated as, 'Attaining Mindfulness by Breathing In and Out' [54], and the title describes exactly its central emphasis.

Even a brief outline of the practice gives an indication of the unexpected breadth of its scope. We start by noticing the difference between our experience of the in-breath and our experience of the out-breath, followed by a similar focusing of our attention on the difference between long breaths and short breaths. We then continue to maintain this awareness of the details of our breathing as we focus in turn on our bodily sensations, our feelings, our state of mind and finally on insights arising from seeing the breath as a key example of the *impermanence* of all our experiences. [55].

The in-and-out rhythm of the breath is a continually changing process, reminding us that all our experiences are also continually changing. My personality, my thoughts, my current state of mind, my feelings, my opinions, my relationships, my possessions; trees, flowers, even the earth itself: everything is changing: things are not fixed or static, although I may sometimes think they are, or even wish they were. Also, by focusing first on the in-breath and then on the out-breath, our sense of the impermanence of things is further enhanced because clearly the moment of the in-breath is 'incomplete' without the moment of the out-breath and vice-versa. So, we are continually reminded that this phase of the breath here-and-now is 'moving on' to the next.

Moreover, by reminding us that our experiences have the form of an on-going flux rather than a static structure, this 'In-and-Out Breathing Meditation' goes on to remind us (in its final stages) that since our experiences are in a continuous state of change, we need not feel 'bound to them'; it is inevitable that we will change and we can experience this inevitability as a liberation, because we can 'let go' of whatever may currently be unhelpful.

This has an interesting political implication. Our politicians may seem to be implying that the choices they are currently offering exhaust all available possibilities. But we can *free* ourselves from this pressure by *letting go* of the assumptions that are being urged upon us and thereby increase our sense of what is possible. And, similarly, we could hope that by engaging in meditation politicians might become able to let go some of the assumptions underlying what they seem currently determined to urge upon the population.

The Body

Just as with the breath, the initial focus in this section is a heightened from of *concentration*. As a start, we engage in what is often called a 'body-scan', where we focus our attention on the different parts of the body in turn, (limbs, joints, organs) just noticing in each case what *sensations* we are aware of. As we notice aches, twinges, itches or even pain, we try to maintain a state of acceptance, rather than avoidance. Sometimes we wait for a particular sensation to change or cease, following the principle of *impermanence* mentioned in the previous section. And sometimes we can simply transfer our awareness to a part of the body where we are currently experiencing no discomfort. The aim is not just to 'relax' the body but to 'become fully acquainted' with how it is here-and-now, rather than, as we usually do, taking it for granted as a sort of vehicle that exists simply to transport 'me' (i.e., my mind and my feelings etc) from place to place.

The term 'Mindfulness' is commonly used to sum up the special form of attention that we are aiming at in meditation; and awareness of the body is one of the 'Ways of Establishing Mindfulness' described at length in an important early Buddhist teaching [56]. The section on the body encourages us to focus our attention on the way that the body is continually changing and, in particular, how it is subject to gradual decay and eventual disintegration.

This is another reminder of the *impermanence* of all our experiences, which has already been mentioned, but with the added purpose of inducing in us an awareness of the delusions involved in perceiving the body as an object of desire. This is not just an implicit warning against personal vanity, but more generally an insight into the problem of *craving*. That our own human body is in a continuous process of decay reminds us dramatically that the same is true of most aspects of our experience. And yet we are easily distracted from this awareness: the depersonalised youthful body is a universally marketed commodity used as a symbolic expression of all the dimensions of egotistical *possessiveness* that cause us so much wasted effort, so much anxiety, and, in the end, so much distress.

But underlying the principle of impermanence there is always the positive, *liberating* message that we are not determined or fixed – that we have the capacity to change. The world of our experience is a system where *everything* changes in response to changing conditions. If we can fully accept that our bodies are inevitably subject to changing conditions, perhaps we can see our wealth, our possessions and our careers in the same light. In this way we can accept that instead of clinging to our opinions, our judgements and our ambitions, as fixed elements that define our being, we can become more *receptive* to new thoughts, and also allow ourselves to be modified by changing conditions, including the opinions, choices and judgements of others.

We can think of the body as being a sort of all-inclusive 'sense organ', registering external as well as internal physical sensations. So, cultivating concentrated awareness of physical sensations also applies to paying very close attention to what we register at a particular point in time with senses such as sight, smell, hearing and touch. There is an important teaching in one of the earliest texts, which clarifies succinctly the relationship between this focus on our physical experiences and a key element in the purpose of meditation practice.

What Bahiya Was Told

Bahiya, a highly respected spiritual teacher living at a great distance from The Buddha and his followers, was starting to wonder whether or not he was close to becoming 'Fully Enlightened'. He was advised to go and consult The Buddha, and so Bahiya set out to walk the eight hundred miles to where the Buddha was staying. On arriving, he immediately asked the Buddha, in the usual way, for 'a teaching'. The Buddha, knowing how far Bahiya had travelled and knowing also that Bahiya was already well advanced in understanding and wisdom, decided that all Bahiya needed was a single piece of advice. This was: he should train himself to experience *"In the seen...merely what is seen, in the heard...merely what is heard, in the sensed...merely what is sensed"*[57]

What is important, in other words, is to avoid responding to an experience by immediately getting caught up in pondering different interpretations. This is traditionally described as *'proliferating'* – a term which nicely reminds us that when our mind lacks the focus that arises from meditation practice it can get enmeshed in endless and unhelpful complexities.

Politically this is particularly important when the complexity involves self-serving justifications and denials, at the expense of straightforward issues of justice and suffering.

Directing (Our) Awareness

So far, the terms 'concentration' and 'focus' have been used to refer to the 'action' dimension of meditation. A more literal (and equally widely used) description of the *act* of meditating is 'directing our awareness'. This phrase is particularly apt in that it reminds us of our capacity for mental and emotional 'agency': sometimes we tend to think that our experience is simply what we 'become aware of' as it unfolds before our senses as a series of ideas or images. But there is another process, which involves *deciding to pay attention* to one element in our awareness of what is going on, leaving other elements as background. Thus, as indicated above, we are able to pay attention to the breath or different physical sensations and to relegate 'distracting' thoughts, plans, memories and anxieties to the background of our consciousness.

There is nothing mysterious about this: we only have to think of those pictorial images which we can just as easily perceive as a vase or as two faces in profile (one as background and the other as foreground), or the occasions when we routinely apologise because we 'didn't notice' something that, we now realise, we *could* have noticed. In other words, any moment of experience includes a number of different elements, but very often one or other of these elements dominates our awareness with a certain psychological 'force', perhaps because it is familiar or obvious and is therefore conventionally what we expect. Whereas in meditation we practise our capacity to direct our awareness to *any* aspect of an experience that we choose; and in this way we are enabled to practise our ability *to dissent* from the familiar and the obvious, and thereby to *question* what otherwise we may feel under pressure (cultural or even political pressure perhaps) to take for granted.

Mindfulness

The act of directing our attention towards a particular object in our experience is one important aspect of 'mindfulness'. 'Mindfulness' has been an important background accompaniment in the discussion so far, and the time has come to bring it centre stage for detailed consideration. Perhaps the most familiar dimension of mindfulness is what is often called 'bare attention' – concentrating the mind by cultivating an intensely focused and entirely non-judgemental state of awareness [58]. The teaching given to Bahiya presents this with radical clarity: perceiving 'in the seen, merely what is seen; in the heard, merely what is heard, etc', and thereby avoiding endlessly 'proliferating' interpretations. The potential value of 'bare attention' is clear: we are trying to bypass our 'habits of mind', our 'self-interest' and judgements that are 'bound up with a preconceived sense of ourselves' [59]. (No need to emphasise how helpful it might be if we all practised this as a response to *political* events!)

But although this perspective on the value of concentrated 'bare attention' seems quite straightforward, it becomes more difficult the more we think about it. Indeed, we might think that Bahiya should have responded to The Buddha's teaching by asking, "But how *exactly* am I supposed to do that? As soon as I notice something I can't help responding with an interpretation of what I think it is, even if this is only a simple act of recognition. How can I possibly stop myself from doing that?" [60]

It is important to note, therefore that there are other dimensions to the practice of mindfulness, beyond this radical refusal to interpret (i.e., 'bare attention'); and these will be considered later. But first, as regards Bahiya's immediate problem, one practical suggestion is to respond to any experience, by focusing on, and repeating many times, the question, "What is this?" In asking the question we are not seeking an answer, but trying to 'open' ourselves' ('without defining anything') to 'the *totality* of what [we] are experiencing at this moment'. Practising this general, open-ended and prolonged questioning can provide a satisfyingly active way of engaging with this rather enigmatic 'pure awareness' aspect of mindfulness. In accepting that the question does not need, and in fact cannot have, a real answer, we breathe in an acceptance that this particular experience, like so much of our experience is just 'perplexing' [61], reminding us of how little we understand and in a final step, instead of feeling that our perplexity is an obstacle, we try to experience it as a liberation – letting go of our usual feeling that, in any given situation, we need to 'know the answer'.

The second aspect of mindfulness is derived from the link between the meaning of the word for mindfulness (*'sati'*) and 'memory'. This aspect of mindfulness is therefore a state of awareness in which we *recollect* the various teachings that make up our overall understanding, in order that we can bring relevant teachings to mind in response to our experiences as they occur. The teachings we need above all to recollect are the ethical and psychological principles that enable to us to discriminate 'wholesome' (skilful, helpful) actions from those that are harmful and destructive [62.]

This process of applying our understanding of general principles to our current experience of events (so far called simply 'recollection') has also been called 'reflexivity' or 'bending back' [63]. 'Bending back' ('re-flex-ing') describes quite graphically the process of focussing as precisely as we can on the 'subjective' dimension of all our experience. In other words, our consciousness doesn't simply register or *mirror* events in the outside world; what we think of as an 'observation' is always our own *interpretation*, in the light of who we are and everything we know. This is inevitable. We have no access to an external, objective world, except through our own experience of it – our senses, our thoughts and our feelings. To recognise this is an essential element of mindfulness: i.e., seeing that the most crucial aspect of our reality (the reality of ourselves, of others, and of the world we all inhabit) is that we are all engaged in 'constructing' it for ourselves, moment by moment.

As an idea, this is not unfamiliar. But as a practice, as a habit, as a state of being it is a big challenge: one of our deepest assumptions and dearest beliefs is that we exist objectively in an objective world. And yet in the practice of mindfulness we have to combine a radically 'reflexive' awareness (of our subjectivity) with the dimension of mindfulness we examined earlier, i.e., trying to experience things 'just as they are'.

'But these two dimensions of mindfulness contradict each other!' I hear you cry. Yes, I reply, but not quite completely. The concentrated *practice* of mindfulness consists precisely in 'living with' this tension, directing our attention to the implicit ambiguity, sinking into it fully with the breath, and *unifying* our experience around it. I can embrace my experience of this moment exactly as it seems to be, leaving nothing out; and yet I am aware that this is *my* experience and no one else's: it will change and so will I.

Moreover, rather than feeling downcast by the obvious difficulties created for us by the tension between these two dimensions of mindfulness, let us not forget the reassurance offered by a third aspect of mindfulness that has not yet been taken into account: the link between mindfulness and a sense of *benevolence, generosity, and our interconnectedness* with all other beings.

Mindfulness, as it has been presented so far, is our comprehensive *understanding* of each experience *just as it is,* in the light of all the teachings that we can recollect. However, one of the most important teachings (which we must therefore *always* recollect!) is that our experiences are permanently in danger of being 'poisoned' by three more or less universal human tendencies: delusion, 'craving' (excessive, unfocussed desire, i.e., 'greed') and animosity. And the practice of mindfulness is, as much as anything else, our continual attempt to counteract these tendencies in ourselves, as we encounter them [64]. As long as we are managing to sustain our mindfulness we will, firstly, be able to avoid the delusion of our separateness from others and our self-centred view of the social world. Secondly, we will be able to recognise impulses of craving/greed in our personal desires and in our dealings with others. Thirdly, we will be able to avoid animosity, i.e., an unfocussed anger that we have not fully analysed, and is therefore not within our control – an anger that we therefore direct not only towards others but also, frequently, towards ourselves.

It is in this last point that we can find consolation for the difficulties that we have encountered in our exploration of mindfulness so far. Because it suggests a key principle of mindfulness (and of meditation generally), namely: *'We need (also) to be kind to ourselves.'* In meditation our long-term aim is always in some way to change things in general for the better, but our immediate aim is simply to get to know ourselves by paying close attention to our experience. And from that point of view there is no point in our habit of *blaming ourselves or becoming angry with ourselves because of our perceived failure.* If our meditation is in some way 'disappointing', this is, rather than 'failure', just another opportunity to learn something about ourselves that we didn't know before.

And as for politics: a radical sense of being connected with others; *questioning* our sense that we already know the answer or that we *ought* to know the answer; interrupting impulses of self-centred craving (e.g., for wealth, power, influence, reputation); analysing critically impulses of anger in order to develop more effective strategies: what could be more helpful?

'Cultivating Kindness'

I know: it sounds a bit sentimental. But there are definite reasons for both words. In meditation we are trying gradually to change our habitual ways of thinking and feeling, but we can't do this by a simple decision or an act of will. Instead, we imitate the *gardener's* activity of 'cultivation' – assembling all the various *favourable conditions* necessary for the eventual 'flowering' of, in this case, an increase in our kindness towards others and towards ourselves. 'Kindness' is a minimal version of all the translations we might choose for one of the most important terms in meditation practice and in Buddhism generally, where it has a similar role in many ways to 'Love' in Christianity. In the original (Pali) language the word is *metta*. '*Metta*' is not usually translated by 'Love', however, partly because of misleading Christian associations, and also because of its equally misleading cultural link with erotic romance. Instead, we can choose between 'Loving kindness', 'kindliness', 'universal well-wishing', 'universal benevolence' and so on; and there is also a close link with the idea of friendship. Or we can solve the problem simply by using the original word un-translated!

To give a sense of the real scope of the term, here is an extract from an important early text, The '*Metta Sutta*' (i.e., 'The Buddha's Teaching on *Metta*'):

"Whatever living beings there be: feeble or strong, tall, stout or medium, short, small or large, without exception; seen or unseen, those dwelling far or near, those who are born or those who are to be born, may all beings be happy!

Let none deceive another, nor despise any person whatsoever in any place. Let him not wish any harm to another out of anger or ill-will.

Just as a mother would protect her only child at the risk of her own life, even so, let him cultivate a boundless heart towards all beings.

Let his thoughts of boundless love pervade the whole world: above, below and across without any obstruction, without any hatred, without any enmity.

Whether he stands, walks, sits or lies down, as long as he is awake, he should develop this mindfulness."[65]

So how do we set about 'cultivating' *metta*? The text gives us a helpful hint, in that it presents abstract ideas by means of vivid details. For example: the whole of humanity becomes 'tall, stout or medium', etc., and unsparing universal devotion becomes the image of a mother's self-sacrifice for an only child. Similarly, in the meditation practice of cultivating *metta* we try to visualise a carefully chosen sequence of people; and in our visualisations (of each person in turn), we try to make each one as vivid as possible so that it can engage our feelings and emotions.

The traditional sequence of visualisations for a meditation to cultivate *metta* was set out in the fifth century by Buddhaghosa [66]. The basic plan is that in the course of the meditation we gradually extend outwards the circle of our 'well-wishing', our feelings of kindliness and empathy towards others. We start with ourselves, and this is absolutely crucial. Many of us have had experiences, in childhood and later, that have left a residue of guilt, anxiety and self-doubt; and we are all shaped by a general culture of competition and consequently an awareness of potential failure and inadequacy. So, we often experience considerable difficulty in simply wishing well towards ourselves.

The second stage is easier. We bring to mind the image of a good friend, and try to experience fully our feelings of affection and appreciation. The third stage is particularly interesting. We visualise someone who we do not *know,* but whose face is familiar to us in some way (perhaps someone we see every day at the bus stop or someone who regularly serves us in a shop, the person who delivers our post or newspapers, etc.). This is someone for whom we have no feelings (positive or negative) and yet who is definitely a member of our social landscape. Traditionally this person is described as 'neutral', but the issue is sharpened if we use the term to describe our response as 'indifference'; and this makes clear the important role this stage can play in our meditation. We want to *move away from our indifference* by cultivating feelings of solidarity, recognising our common humanity, our shared hopes and sufferings; by experiencing fully, in other words, that they are 'the same as us'. The ethical significance of this stage is very clear, as is its potential value as a critical perspective on many aspects of political life.

The same is true of the fourth stage, where we visualise someone with whom our current relationship is somewhat difficult, towards whom we tend to feel a degree of animosity or irritation – perhaps because of their opinions or perhaps because something about them just seems to 'rub us up the wrong way'.

In the fifth stage of the meditation, loving kindness is extended to the whole world, as the *'Metta Sutta'* clearly anticipates. Thus, we extend the circle of solidarity celebrating our common humanity, by including *anyone* at all that has recently made a strong impression on us. This might include people we have met or just seen in passing or read about or seen on TV – as long as our awareness of them is vivid enough to have created an emotional element (positive or negative) in our response [67]. (This aspect of the meditation process is described in more detail in the next section, on the role of the imagination.)

Changing our feelings (from indifference or irritation to kindliness) is of course exactly what seems really difficult. However, a solution is at hand, because at this point, we can make use of a very helpful distinction that is always made in traditional Buddhist teachings. This is the distinction between a feeling as an *impulse* and a feeling as a process that exists for a period of time, i.e., what we call an *emotion*[68]. Our initial impulse is simply a positive, negative or neutral reaction, but this usually goes on to determine what sort of conscious emotion eventually arises. However, given this distinction (between an emotional impulse and an emotional state), we can see that in principle there is always a small 'time gap' between the two, between the initial impulse and the eventual emotion. It is during this gap that we have a brief opportunity to *choose* how to respond, i.e., to respond 'creatively', in a way that is *liberated'* from our initial impulse. And this reminds us that in one of the early texts a stage of meditation that begins with 'contemplating' the mind culminates in *liberating* the mind [69].

It is tempting to imagine how helpful it would be if we could all 'liberate' ourselves in this way from our immediate 'impulsive' reactions to what people say and do. We can speculate on how it could transform us as individuals, what effect it might have on our relationships, and also on our responses to events in the world of politics. Perhaps we could develop a habit of noticing and questioning our impulses of indifference towards fellow citizens, and also try to minimise the intensity of our feelings of animosity towards those we interpret as being (actually or potentially) our political opponents.

Imagining Others

The form of practice described in the previous section (i.e., cultivating a more 'kindly response to others' lives through a process of *visualisation)* is very similar to what we may think of as the workings of our *imagination.* As the word itself implies, the imagination brings into our mind a visual *image* of something or someone not present. The imagination in this sense is the creative faculty of our humanity, enabling us to make vivid and present an experience that had previously been only an abstraction or a possibility. Also, it is our imagination that helps us to appreciate fully our impermanence, i.e., to imagine things being other than they are, including imagining our own absence; and thus, to envisage in general the possibility of change.

But at this point I think I hear a sceptical reaction, such as: 'I'm just trying to feel a bit kinder towards people and not lose my temper in political meetings; I'm not trying to write a poem or a novel!' But what about the following observations by the poet Shelley as he proposes a use of the imagination which is very reminiscent of the meditation practices described in the previous section? Shelley writes:

"Human beings, to be greatly good, must imagine intensely and comprehensively; they must put themselves in the place of others...and of many others; the pains and pleasures of their species must become their own the great instrument of the moral good is the imagination." [70]

For Shelley, 'the moral good' is putting oneself in the place of others; and thus, implicitly transcending the egotistical self-centred view of the world which so often circumscribes our awareness. But this could describe not only the work of the imagination (which is Shelley's point) but, equally, one of the key purposes of meditation, as well as one of the central teachings of Buddhism. Indeed, it is illustrated in one of Buddhism's favourite stories, the story of Kisa-Gotami [71].

The Story of Kisa-Gotami

Ever since she was a little child Gotami was much thinner than the other girls, and as a result she had to put up with the insulting nickname 'Kisa-Gotami' (i.e., 'Skinny' Gotami). And then, on top of that, when she got married her husband treated her badly, so it was only when she bore a child that at last people started to treat her with some respect. However, just when her little boy was old enough to begin to run about and play, he became ill and died. At this point Gotami, overwhelmed by her grief, refused to believe that he was dead. So she took the little corpse from house to house, asking for medicine to cure her child. "Why are you asking for medicine?" everyone said. "Can't you see that the child is dead?"

But one of her neighbours, wiser and more kindly than the others, realised that Gotami's strange behaviour was due to the depth of her sorrow, and said: "Why don't you go to the Buddha; perhaps he can help you". So, she took the dead body of her little boy, showed it to the Buddha, and said, "Please give me some medicine for my poor sick child." The Buddha looked at Gotami and at the little dead body; and he said to her, "Go back to the town, knock on all the doors and wherever you find a household where no one has died ask them to give you a little mustard seed. Then bring me all the mustard seed you collect and we will make a medicine for your child."

So Gotami went into the town, still carrying the dead body of her little boy, knocked on the door of the first house and said, "If no one has died in your family, please give me some mustard seed: I need it as a medicine for my sick child." The woman of the house looked at her sadly and said, "Certainly I can give you some mustard seed, but I'm afraid that we have had many, many deaths in our family." And Gotami replied, "In that case, your mustard seed will be of no use as medicine for my little boy." She went to the second house, and the same thing happened: yes, she could have some mustard seed, but in that house also there had been many deaths and much sorrow. And at the third, fourth and fifth house, and at every house where she knocked at the door, it was the same story: the family were in sorrow for the death of a dearly loved relative – a mother, or a father, or an uncle, or an aunt, or a son, or a daughter.

By the evening, she still had no mustard seed for medicine for her child. However, something important had happened. As a result of sharing her sorrow with so many other people who also had lost a loved one, she found that the nature of her own sorrow had changed. No longer did she simply feel agonised by her own feelings. Instead, although she still felt grief at the loss of her child, she also knew that there were many others in the town who had also experienced a similar loss and the same terrible sorrow. She realised that sorrow and death are part of how life is, not only for her but for everyone. So, she took her dead child to the cemetery outside the town and buried him – with sorrow, but now also with wisdom and compassion. And from that time onwards, Gotami became one of the wisest and most respected followers of the Buddha.

So, following both Shelley and the Buddhist story of Kisa-Gotami, we can associate the exercise of our imagination with our capacity for transcending a self-centred view of the world, i.e., developing our capacity for empathy with the experience of others. This brings us to a further important teaching on the nature of *metta,* which identifies different forms of *metta* [72] by describing how in different situations our feelings are the result of different types of imaginative action, and involve directing our attention towards a different aspect of our experience. In this light, then, let us revisit the five stages of 'Cultivating Kindliness' described in the previous section and the issues that may arise in the different stages.

We sometimes experience difficulty in the first stage, (cultivating kindliness towards ourselves) because the vicissitudes of our lives may have left us with a tendency to anxiety, self-doubt, anger and guilt, which can surface when we start to meditate. However, one of the origins of our self-doubt may be that we are blaming ourselves for something because of the fantasy assumption that others are blaming us. In other words, we may be unnecessarily placing ourselves at the centre of a situation where in fact the others involved are probably pre-occupied with their own issues. Whereas if we try to *imagine* what those other people's issues might be, we may well start to experience a helpful sense of relief and connectedness.

In the second stage (cultivating feelings of appreciation towards a good friend) our imaginative action is that of enjoying without reservation the *happiness or success of others*. But that 'without reservation' is crucial. It reminds us that our generous appreciation of our friend's success can be undermined by other motives (envy, for example, alas!) so that although our aim is, in Shelley's words, to 'put [ourselves] in the place of others', we don't always manage to do so.

And then there' is *compassion*. Again, there is a possibility that our imaginative efforts towards reacting with generosity and empathy to someone's *suffering* (physical or emotional) may be insufficient; and may, again, include a self-centred impulse. So that instead of putting ourselves in the place of the person who is suffering in order to understand what sort of support they would appreciate, we stay firmly in our own place, not wanting to get too close, for example, because we don't want our own mood to be 'brought down'.

The emphasis is rather different in the third stage, as we meditate on the familiar stranger. Precisely through the absence of a personal relationship we rely on our imagination to intensify our response from merely a 'neutral' interest ('indifference') to an act of emotional identification, starting from our visualisation of the particular individual but generalising out to an awareness of what Shelley calls "the pains and pleasures of our species." This also suggests how the imagination is not only, as Shelley says, a force for 'the moral good' but also politically significant.

Similarly when we meditate in the fourth stage on the person who is currently causing us irritation. Instead of seeing the situation from the point of view of my own irritation ('X is irritating me') can I imagine it in terms of X's experience? Difficult, of course; but I could *imagine* that in X's life there may be suffering (grief, bereavement, physical pain) that I am unaware of, which is affecting the way X behaves towards me. This is cause for regret, and if possible, sympathy, but certainly not cause for irritation. Perhaps indeed, freed from irritation, I might be able to imagine something positive I could actually say or do.

The dimension of *metta,* usually described as being the culmination of all the others, is *equanimity* [73] – a form of imaginative action demanding all the qualities of the other three: universal benevolence empathy and compassion. As such it entails a response that combines intensity with emotional *balance* and a *comprehensive* awareness of the manifold possibilities and implications of a situation. This is particularly helpful in the fifth stage of the meditation. Here we visualise 'anyone' who happens to have recently made an impact on us – someone we have met or read about or seen on TV. Thus, during our meditation we may expand our awareness such that we feel emotionally and politically inspired as we identify with people exemplifying courage and altruism – doctors and nurses in war zones or disaster areas.

But we may ask, what role does the imagination play when we become intensely aware of examples, local or worldwide, of inequality, destitution, brutality, oppression, and injustice? We might answer tentatively that our imagination enables us to identify simultaneously with human experience *as a whole* (in other words, as Shelley suggested: 'the pains and pleasures of *our species*'). It often seems more natural to respond immediately to a *single* aspect of a situation and to temporarily ignore the others, e.g., by focusing only on examples of unselfish heroism, or only on injustice and suffering, or feeling despair when we contemplate our helplessness with respect to both. In contrast, the imagination is the means by which we reach our most *comprehensive* response to events – energetically *balancing and synthesising* all the relevant factors – events, motives, feelings – that we can think of: admiration for the possibilities of human courage; compassion for the suffering of so many as a result of injustices and disasters; and compassion even for those whose humanity has been so distorted that they have been led into large-scale actions of cruelty. In other words, our imagination always *integrates and extends* our understanding – of the human capacity for devotion and fortitude, and also of how those we must condemn may, at the same time, be victims of their circumstances.

'The Unconscious'

In seeking to clarify the distinction between meditation and 'thinking about something' it is useful to remind ourselves of the familiar idea that our consciousness has different *levels*. The everyday business of life bobs along 'on the surface', so to speak; while at a 'deeper' level, in what we often call 'the unconscious', some experiences are somehow 'hidden', until they come to the surface in dreams, accidents, 'slips' of the tongue, 'random' association of ideas, 'sudden' memories, or 'unexpected' impulses. Thus, it is often claimed that the power of meditation practice enables us to make contact with ideas or emotions that have been somehow forgotten or 'buried', and for that very reason may be helpful because they will be new and unfamiliar. The practical methods whereby we gain access to these buried thoughts and feelings are those outlined in previous sections: breathing, focusing, directing our awareness, visualising and imagining, enabling us to cultivate concentration and compassion.

But suppose we contact such 'unconscious' thoughts and emotions, what happens then? How is it supposed to help us? What sort of process is involved? The psychologist Guy Claxton refers to the unconscious as a set of widespread but highly misleading delusions about our experience, and in particular about what will make us happy. We are therefore vulnerable to a sense of 'unease' when 'reality', in his words, 'does break though' (i.e., when we realise that our delusions *are* delusions); and he agrees that when that happens the various Buddhist meditation methods can he used to 'sort it out' [74].

The suggestion that our conventional state of being is one of delusion is an important traditional Buddhist teaching. However, there is an interesting twist: 'delusion' is often used interchangeably with 'ignorance' [75], reminding us that our ignorance is not simply an accidental absence of knowledge but the result of a much deeper problem: the 'poisoning' of all our experiences by our habitual responses of greed and anger [76], as mentioned earlier. Thus, the relationship of our meditation practice to experiences of which we are not usually conscious is more than a process of 'breaking through' and 'sorting out'. Rather, we are awakened from our state of ignorant delusion, greed and anger when we concentrate, direct and integrate our awareness; so that we can cultivate our capacity for kindness, compassion and interconnectedness with other beings.

In contrast, when we turn to the Buddhist teaching on 'Alaya', the function of the unconscious in the practice of meditation is given a rather more straightforward description:

"The *alaya* or storehouse consciousness is the Buddhist equivalent of the unconscious mind. It is like a garden, in which every experience and action sows a seed which may later sprout and create our unfolding life." [77]

So, the 'storehouse consciousness' contains the 'seeds' deposited by all our actions, positive *and* negative, rather like hidden memories of our past. They remain below the threshold of our conscious awareness, but continue to affect our behaviour in positive and negative ways, depending on the nature of the original actions. In meditation we 'rest' in this level of consciousness by *visiting* our storehouse of remembered actions, just noticing 'what is there', accepting and trusting what our attention is bringing to us, without comparison or judgement [78].

Alternatively, we can take 'Buddha Nature' as our model of the unconscious, where the deepest level of our being is taken to be *entirely* positive. Three qualities define the basic impulses of our Buddha Nature: '*openness*' (a capacity for well-being arising from a sense of our potential 'spaciousness', a sense that the vitality and scope of our being has no limit), *clarity* (a capacity for 'awareness', i.e., for understanding fully the nature of our experience), and *sensitivity* (a capacity for feeling connected with others, for generosity and compassion). Given that the positive qualities of Buddha Nature are potentially present in *all* of us, our meditation practice is a process of moving away from our usual socially conditioned, egotistical and distorted perception of our experience, and developing instead a confidence in the 'intrinsic worth' of ourselves and all others [79].

It might be objected that this account of a Buddha Nature buried within each of us seems at the very least to rely on a somewhat one-sided optimism without supporting evidence. So, we may be tempted to ask, is this then simply a matter of faith? However, from even the simplest evolutionary perspective, human beings have always needed the ability to empathise and co-operate with other members of their primary group in order to survive [80]. And so, we have quite good reason to suppose that the qualities of a Buddha Mind something like those outlined above are likely to exist somewhere in our being, and that our meditation practice can re-discover them. Indeed, some aspects of the public response to the Covid-19 crisis of 2020–21 (voluntary support for vulnerable members of the community, exchanging smiles as we make space for each other on pathways as we walk) gives support to this optimism.

However, as individuals we are of course influenced by the social world we inhabit. Hence, the elements in our individual unconscious will be not only the 'seeds' of our own lives and our various 'intrinsic capacities' but also the *myths* or 'archetypes' derived from our culture, embodying universal dimensions of human experience [81]. In many ways an archetype is simply a general idea or image to which human beings have always regularly attached great significance. Examples might be: the mother figure, the father figure, the vulnerable child, the hero, the villain, the tempter, the wise old man or woman, the journey to seek fortune or truth, and so on. We can see them embodied in novels, drama, folk tales and nursery stories. Sangharakshita comments:

'In Buddhism it is always clearly...stated that all these appearances, all these archetypal forms, are ultimately...projections from our own unconscious, and that they are to be integrated... One cannot really resolve an archetype in the sense of incorporating it into one's conscious mind...unless one realises that...it isn't something objectively existing, but something which one has projected from some depths, from some hidden source within oneself' [82].

If we become aware, during meditation, of something that has 'archetypal' significance for us, this suggests that it is a significant emotional element in our lives. Our meditation *practice* might then involve trying to 'integrate' that element fully into the rest of our experience, using a sequence of visualisations, the breath, etc. From the point of view of meditation, one particularly interesting archetype is 'The Shadow' [83], i.e., an aspect of ourselves that we try to avoid 'owning up to', and where the process of accepting and integrating is therefore particularly challenging.

Moreover, it can be argued that in politics also the intellectual and emotional landscape is partly created by myths and archetypes. We might simply point to the very general and simplified form of the rival ideologies put forward by political parties and amplified by the media. Obvious examples are: 'Freedom of Speech'; 'The Rule of Law'; 'The Welfare State'; 'Free Enterprise'; 'The People'; 'The Establishment'; 'Institutional Racism'; National Culture'; 'Immigrants'; 'Scroungers', etc. By means of these and similar terms *'The political unconscious'* constructs the social world in which we think, speak and interact 'in our own cultural and practical experience.' [84]

The terms listed above are derived from familiar issues and debates in our political culture. In other political cultures, the dominant myths will be different, based on tribal or religious confrontations, for example. But in any case, a political culture based on debate and opposition will always create such myths and archetypes in an attempt to impose some sort of coherence and logic onto its inevitable ambiguities and contradictions. [85] (The four concepts analysed in Chapter Two could also be seen in this light.) The point is that further thought (and repeated meditation) can often reveal that in the end these archetypal terms, tempting as they undoubtedly are because of their familiarity, are too simple to provide a basis for a proper understanding of our social and political world. Instead, we can advance our understanding by contacting their 'hidden source' in our experience and our emotions, and thereby (to use the words of Sangharakshita quoted earlier) 'resolve' and 'integrate' them into the forms of awareness, understanding, and compassion we so urgently need.

Summary

In this chapter I have argued that we can 'be the change we want to see in the world' by *directing our attention*, i.e., re-focussing our thoughts and our feelings in ways that are helpful; not only directly to us as individuals, as friends or as members of a family, but also potentially as members of a political culture: as electors, journalists, campaigners, councillors, members of parliament, and members of a government or its opposition.

In order to suggest how the practice of meditation can bring about this refocusing of our attention, I have needed to explain the methods of meditation in terms of the teachings from which they are derived; but I have tried to do so without suggesting that meditation relies on a particular 'faith' – other than our confidence in the effectiveness of meditation itself.

Looking back over the different sections, I have emphasised the role of practising *concentration*, especially by means of directing our awareness towards a specific object, including our breathing, and through practising intense *awareness* of the details of our experience through visualisation. In particular, meditation enables us to experience (emotionally as well as intellectually) the *impermanence* of all our experiences, leading to a sense of *freedom* that we can *let go* of some of our apparently fixed opinions and assumptions and also those that are being urged upon us by the political culture in which we live.

Other politically valuable experiences that can arise as we practice meditation include: a radical sense of *being connected with others*; the habit of regularly *questioning* our sense that in any given situation we already ready know the answer; managing to *interrupt impulses of self-centred craving* (e.g., for wealth, power, influence, reputation); and *noticing impulses of anger* – so that we can try to minimise the intensity of feelings of animosity – including, for example, towards political opponents in order to engage more effectively with their policies. In general, meditation involves extending outwards our capacity for appreciating friends, to include strangers and those whose activities we may object to or even deplore. One quality that this ideal of ethical and political inclusivity evokes is our capacity for *imagination,* enabling us to keep a comprehensive *balance* between *all* the competing and contradictory aspects of how we experience and understand a situation – those that may inspire us or horrify us or leave us mourning our helplessness.

Finally, in all aspects of our lives, including our experience of politics, we find ourselves trying to make sense of events, situation, and people in terms of stereotypes derived from a culture of politically and emotionally charged myths. And through meditation we can see their limitations and minimise their influence over our thinking and our political responses, as we notice how they arise as projections of our individual hopes and fears.

In the next chapter the full argument for the potential importance of meditation for our political life is drawn together.

A more detailed account of the specific practices involved in meditation is given in the final chapter 'A Practical Guide to Meditation Methods'.

Chapter Four
Meditation: Mindfulness, Education and Politics

So where are we, in terms of establishing specifically *political* benefits from meditation practice? Let us start by considering the following summary, based on the analysis in Chapter Three and the references to meditation in Chapter Two.

The first point, clearly, is *concentration* – the ability to *focus* our otherwise frequently scattered mental energy. The phrase 'directing our awareness' makes clear that this entails an *action,* and indeed a repeated series of actions, because it doesn't always work! By directing our awareness toward the *momentary sensations* of the body and the details of our breathing, for example, we become more generally able to see events simply 'in themselves', rather than enmeshed with our usual convoluted mixture of anxieties, self-interested desires, and denials.

Our acts of concentration focus equally on the state of our *thoughts* and the state of our *feelings.* Some of these will be surprising, unwelcome and even painful, and in this way, we become aware of the need to *integrate* negative aspects of our experience with other element in our awareness, and to avoid the temptation to deny them or project them onto others.

Concentrating on what we are experiencing within the present moment enables us to realise that everything is part of a general process of change. There are two main implications here: first, the *impermanence* of *all* our experiences – including our own thoughts, feelings, opinions and responses to other people – and, second, our *connectedness* with other beings and forms of life.

By noticing the general principle of *'impermanence'* and training ourselves to be fully aware of the impermanence of our experiences, we find we can hold opinions 'lightly' (rather than dogmatically); we can let go of needing to feel certain that our own current opinion is completely right or indeed that someone else's is completely wrong; and we can accept that our feelings may change in response to new evidence and conditions. Moreover, from this perspective, instead of seeing our current doubts and perplexities as reasons for anxiety, we can, on the contrary, welcome them: they may be the beginnings of *liberation* from current circumstances and assumptions, even though some politicians (and others) may be urging them upon us as inescapable.

By directing our attention towards our *'connectedness'* we train ourselves to recognise that the elements of our experience are not 'things' – fixed and permanent – but 'processes': each in turn part of a universal system of mutually interlocking and continuously changing conditions and circumstances. We are initially reminded of this by each humble breath; and then step-by-step we notice that the same is true of thoughts, feelings, and that interesting phenomenon known as the 'self'. The self (yours and mine and everyone else's) has an apparent separateness' from other 'selves', but on careful consideration all of our individual qualities turn out to be dependent on innumerable causal factors, almost always involving other people. Gradually, our meditation practice impresses on us that our separateness from others is an illusion; and is the origin of egotism, self-centredness, self-importance, possessiveness, and in the end, animosity and aggression. Instead, in meditation we repeatedly visualise the humanity of others, and slowly wean ourselves away from any residual lack of concern for the sufferings of strangers.

We can extend this argument a little, because by noticing intensely the various forms of our connectedness with others, we come to understand more fully the nature of our *responsibility* towards our fellow beings. Each of our actions is the start of a chain-reaction of others' reactions, spreading out in a ripple effect whose details and limits we cannot predict or calculate. Our sense of responsibility for the effects of our actions is therefore something that (in the absence of precise knowledge) we have to construct and interpret. And we are required therefore to visualise the scope of our ethical responsibilities by *imagining* the consequences of our actions, exercising our ability to identify with those in very different circumstances, to 'stand in another's shoes'. And this of course necessarily expands the scope of our thinking about any political policies we may be inclined to adopt or oppose.

But what exactly is this collection of experiences, insights and perspectives? What do they add up to? Are they perhaps the elements of a supposedly 'non-partisan' political ideal? This interesting possibility will be explored later, but first it is important to note that above all, as meditation practices, they describe different *habits* and outcomes arising from habits –

habits that we may have practised in our own way over a lengthy period of time, and which will therefore have become part of the way in which, as individuals, we respond to the world. Or habits that *could be practised* over a period of time and which *could* therefore become part of the way we respond to the world. (Or, if this book is your first introduction to practising meditation, a list of habits that you now, perhaps, seriously intend to start practising!)

They suggest how in a number of ways, through meditation, we can *extend* our awareness so that our perspective becomes more *comprehensive,* less narrowly focused on how the world appears to our personal viewpoint. It suggests a set of habits (or we might even call them 'skills', once they have actually become habits) that, arising from meditation practice, eventually affect our behaviour, both as individuals and in relation to others. So, they can also have various forms of potential political relevance, as outlined in Chapter Three. Precisely *how* they can be understood as having a political relevance is discussed in the final section of this chapter.

Meanwhile it is instructive to consider the political relevance or otherwise of some work that has been done so far to introduce meditation in different institutional settings, starting, appropriately, with the world of politicians, where a considerable effort has gone already into introducing mindfulness and meditation. For example, the 'Mindfulness Initiative' reports that its work currently (2020) involves 250 UK parliamentarians and 14 national parliaments [86]. Here for example are some politicians reflecting on some politically helpful outcomes of their experience of meditation:

'…We'd have a more effective legislation because people would be coming from a more balanced place…' Tony Cardenas, USA [87]

'…There would be a more considered approach to exchanges of differing views' Tim Laughton, UK [88];

"Passionate people go into politics but mindfulness is a way of tempering that passion." Chris Ruane, UK [89].

'Politics' includes more than politicians, of course, so it is important that we consider the institutions where politics interacts with the other dimensions of the social world – business, for example. Here are some comments from chief executives from the world of high finance.

A market trader at Goldman Sachs: "There was this one instance where the market tanked and there was a panic on the desk… Thanks to my meditation practice I was able to keep my composure and propose solutions to reduce the impact of the market crash."

A CEO and entrepreneur: "I didn't tend to understand what my team was going through. I would just get angry if they did not perform according to my expectations… Thanks to meditation I have developed patience."

A CEO facing a disgruntled shareholder: "I paused and slowly took a few breaths… This led me to actually listen and understand not only his situation but what he wanted and expected. By not responding in an emotional manner, it resulted in his becoming not only supportive but also becoming an ally."

CEO of an investment company: "Meditation has helped me discard interesting but unnecessary information and focus on the few things that make a difference to long run investment performance."

The researcher, Emma Seppala, writing in the Harvard Business Review and generalising from these examples, argues that meditation leads to 'focus', 'improves your relationships', 'enhances creativity', 'boosts emotional intelligence', and 'builds resilience' [90].However, we may well feel that all this, although positive enough, is rather limited, in comparison with the list we started with at the beginning of this chapter. In particular, the term 'resilience' has a significant political limitation. It implies that the main advantage of meditation is that it helps us to preserve our ability to (literally) 'bounce back' from our problems. Helpful though this ability may be in certain circumstances, meditation is *also* about practising our capacity for *understanding* our experience *in a wider context* and for acting upon this wider understanding. Hence, the forms of meditation for which I am arguing involve attempting to develop both greater self-awareness and a greater awareness of our social and political environment.

A similar issue arises from the work of Edo Shonin et. al, writing on his research with middle managers'[91].

"Participants demonstrated significant and sustainable improvements over control-group participants in levels of work-related stress, job satisfaction…and employer-rated job performance… Meditation may reduce the separation made by employees between their own interests and those of the organisations they work for."

Again, there seems here to be an emphasis on the role of meditation in encouraging *acceptance* of one's circumstances without a similar emphasis on the dimension of meditation practice summed up as *'critical reflection'* [92] which is implicit in some of the aspects listed at the beginning of this chapter, e.g., on increased openness to alternative perspectives, and an increased awareness of the scope of our responsibilities.

Perhaps the reason for the rather restricted scope of these examples is that the teaching of meditation currently often takes the form of short interventions of a few weeks as part of a therapeutic or research process, for example, the website 'Meditation in Universities: 30 Colleges Lead the Way' turns out to be concerned explicitly with various types of 'meditation for mental health'. This is reminiscent of the 'therapeutic' model of meditation mentioned in Chapter One, derived from pioneering work on the use of meditation to improve the treatment of depression. What is often missing is the recognition that in order to realise the full possibilities of meditation a short programme of 'mindfulness-based therapy' needs to be followed up by continuing regular practice. This is emphasised by Jon Kabat-Zinn himself, the pioneer and originator of the 'therapeutic' model of meditation [93]. And in a recent issue of *New Scientist* the neurologist Steven Laureys reports that it is in the brains of '*long-term* meditators' that beneficial increases in the 'grey matter' (improving memory and attention) can be observed [94].

This is a reminder that only if meditation becomes a *habit* – at the level of our cognitive and emotional responses (rather than something we 'know about'), is it likely to have any significant *political* impact. And what this in turn suggests is that in spite of the increasing recognition of the value of meditation, and without in any way wishing to minimise the value to individuals of its therapeutic benefits, meditation needs to find a central place in the institutions where we can expect lifelong habits to be established, i.e., in *schools*.

'Mindfulness' and 'Meditation' in Schools

As long as school life is not seen just as a process where the young are provided with the skills necessary for employment, but also as a preparation for a life of self-fulfilment, the qualities listed at the beginning of the chapter (roughly: concentration, open-mindedness, ethical self-awareness and empathy) would seem quite appropriate as elements of an educational philosophy. In this respect, meditation is easily placed in a conventional school curriculum, under the heading of 'Citizenship' and/or 'Personal and Social Education', for example; and it has also been introduced, more informally, as a way of beginning and ending periods of study. Thus, there seems to be no obvious reason why meditation could not be started early and sustained over the whole of the educational experience, thereby becoming a culturally widespread habit that informs our response to the world.

Fortunately, it is clear that a lot of work on meditation in schools has already taken place, and is indeed well established. Thomas Armstrong's 2019 book *Mindfulness in the Classroom* reports evidence that school-based programmes have involved 'over 300,000 students in the United States…and over 500,000 students around the world'; and that these have involved the development of *'core competences* [such as] self-awareness, self-management, social awareness, relationship skills and responsible decision-making.' He is optimistic that 'mindfulness practices…can be easily integrated into the [curriculum] initiatives that teachers are already using in their classrooms…can be used as part of the counselling, psychological and social services of a school, and can be integrated into the health education courses in a district.' Armstrong also notes that for meditation sessions to be effective with children, it is important that teachers should first develop their own meditation practice, so that they can 'model' the process as well as teach it. This modelling process is also of course of direct benefit to the teachers themselves, since their own professional experience is often highly stressful, with potentially negative consequences for the education of the students. So, in this way both teachers and students benefit from the teacher's meditation practice [95].

However, Armstrong also indicates some significant problems. He notes the danger that teachers may use 'mindfulness' as a classroom management strategy or even as a punishment: he quotes one teacher as responding to a child who has made a mistake in some maths work by tearing up her paper and saying, "Go to the calm-down chair and sit!" In other words, what may perhaps be called 'meditation' can simply become yet another means for enforcing order. He also notes that some parents may object to their children engaging in meditation because they are afraid it might be a covert form of religious indoctrination. Writing mainly for a readership in the United States, he is very aware that *secularism* in education can be a constitutional issue and that consequently schools may be suspicious of anything that looks like 'Eastern Religion'. This is an important observation, and not only in relation to meditation in a school context. But Armstrong is perhaps rather too cautious in insisting that the term 'mindfulness' must always be used, rather than 'meditation' and in asserting that his model of 'mindfulness' is based *entirely* on experimental neurological evidence showing that mindfulness practices have been shown to change the structure and functioning of the brain [96].

All this explains why Armstrong's account of the teaching of 'mindfulness', based on the 'core competences' mentioned above, is rather limited in scope. And this limitation is above all *political,* as he himself admits:

'Mindfulness may serve as a way of placing the responsibility for societal ills on individual students and not on the broader culture...students are told to accept their anger rather than turn it towards solving social ills such as unsafe neighbourhoods, racial disparities and economic inequity.' [97].

Armstrong's admission is serious. He attempts to remedy the problem by recommending simply that activities intended to promote 'kindness and compassion' should be added to the practice of 'mindfulness', and he emphasises that 'mindfulness and compassion are linked to each other' in the sense that individual 'serenity' leads us to be less 'judgemental' of others [98]. But his various suggestions, while imaginative and adapted to a range of classroom situations, remain some way short of the model of meditation outlined at the beginning of this chapter, which is specifically intended to include substantial political implications.

This tension between broader and narrower interpretations of the scope of meditation as a contribution to education in schools is nothing new. Nearly twenty years earlier, in 2001, a book on meditation in schools with the ominously limiting subtitle 'A Practical Guide to Calmer Classrooms' presented the following list of the 'useful effects of meditation': 'stress management', 'optimum effective learning', 'training attention', and 'learning to be in the present moment' [99]. Whereas, in contrast, the concluding chapter of the same volume proposes a much broader and more critical perspective:

'Introducing meditation...into a school's provision can provide an opportunity to re-conceive the basis of its educational vision. When children are asked to attend to their 'whole selves'...it does not result in conformity but questioning... This can be uncomfortable for schools, teachers and parents, [because] children become empowered to change things and to put into effect their own vision of achievement... Meditation is a key strategy in ensuring that [students] recognise their potential. It is concerned with reflecting upon one's own experience without being caught up in the anxieties, prejudices and attachments that construe our motivations and pronouncements according to our own gains and desires.' [100].

This perspective from school education suggests some key issues as regards the cultural and political role of meditation more generally. Meditation can be (but is not always) a process of critical reflection in which we 're-conceive' our experience without reinforcing either our anxieties or our various forms of self-interested motivation. However, for all of us, not only for the parents and teachers of school students, there is a key question: is our main purpose in meditating to 'fit in' more comfortably with the culture of the world in which we find ourselves, or is it also to support us in 'questioning', extending, and developing our responses to our world, even with some vision of possible social change in view?

The 'therapeutic' model of mindfulness was, as mentioned earlier, originally developed as a treatment for depression, and its main purpose, naturally, was to help us to live more comfortably with the expectations of our everyday roles, i.e., to enable us to respond to them with greater tranquillity in spite of their stress-inducing pressures. In contrast, the model of meditation presented in this book is intended to enable us to *question* certain aspects of the way we experience our social and political world. And this may well be perceived in some quarters – not only schools but universities, businesses corporations and political parties – as 'uncomfortable'. The limited scope of much of the work on meditation, compared with the possibilities outlined listed at the outset of this chapter, is not therefore altogether surprising.

However, this tension between meditation for tranquillity and a form of meditation that emphasises ethical and political *critique* is not one that we necessarily have to resolve. If we want meditation to become an established habit for young children, it needs above all to help them come to terms with themselves and with a highly stress-inducing culture, amidst the strains of 'growing up' and maintaining a satisfactory identity among their peers.

But assuming that this level of self-awareness can be established as a starting point, what then? 'What then?' is the theme of this book: how meditation can also help to gradually create forms of political awareness that increase our autonomy and effectiveness as adult citizens – as friends, as members of a family, as members of the electorate, as members of a profession, as managers, as trade unionists, as chief executives, as members of parliament, and even as members of a government.

Meditation Practices and Political 'Virtues'

But *in what sense* can meditation develop our *political* awareness? This is obviously the key question; it has been implicit in much of the preceding discussion, but now, as the argument moves into its concluding stages, it needs to be made explicit. Can an enhanced form of political awareness and understanding be *inherent in* our practice of meditation? If not, some might object that what has been described as the political 'relevance' of meditation practice has been 'smuggled in'; that under the guise of 'meditation', a partisan critique is being presented, based largely on moral approval/disapproval, or on political ideology. So, what is needed is a clear distinction between, on the one hand, the effects of meditation and, on the other hand, moral or political 'opinions'.

Perhaps this distinction is already implicit in the summary of the habits of mind arising from meditation presented at the beginning of this chapter. Is it? If we check back, the list seems to suggest, innocuously enough, that the habits of meditation lead us to be more concentrated, more imaginative, more objective, more honest, more open-minded, more tolerant of uncertainty, more self-questioning, more optimistic, more appreciative. So far, so good: nothing necessarily controversial or overtly partisan in any of that. But what about the suggestion that meditation leads us to become more aware of our *connectedness* with others, leading directly to a rejection of 'self-centredness' and 'greed', adopting habits of compassion toward strangers, and (consequently) appreciating the enhanced scope of our social *responsibilities.* At first sight, it could be suggested that these are indeed elements of a *moral* agenda or elements of what some might call a 'liberal' political ideology. It is this suggestion that needs to be modified if the general argument presented in this book is to be relevant for readers from a wide variety of political belief and opinion.

The presentation in Chapter Three of these aspects of meditation practice (i.e., connectedness, compassion, etc (see especially sections iv and v) is intended to show that they derive initially *not* from ethical teachings about what we ought to do and how we ought to be, but from very general philosophical and psychological teachings about the nature of our experience. Ethical implications certainly emerge later; but they are not the starting point. The starting point in our meditation practice is simply the act of directing our awareness so that we concentrate on the detail of a particular experience. And the first insight to arise from that concentrated awareness is that all elements of our experience are *impermanent.* We initially experience the principle of impermanence in the succession of one breath after another, and in the arising and ceasing of physical sensations, thoughts and emotions. Subsequently, as our meditation practice develops, as mentioned earlier, we begin to experience with full emotional engagement the impermanence of more significant areas of our lives, i.e., the impermanence of our bodies and our sense of 'self'.

The next step is the important one, in terms of our concern with politics and ethics. (But after a moment's thought we could perhaps see it as it is not only unsurprising but self-evident.) Impermanence is a characteristic of every aspect of our experience, for the 'simple' reason that everything is *linked,* in universal processes of *mutual influence,* and it is this system of interlocking influence which causes changes to occur. In other words, the reason why things don't just 'stay as they are' is because everything is continuously subject to a multitude of conditioning influences. Thus, the other key teaching here is that all of our experiences arise and cease 'in dependence on' particular but innumerable 'conditions'. So, each of our experiences, including the experience of our own sense of self, is essentially and originally bound up in a universal process of 'interdependence' with other events and experiences, including the 'selves' of others. It therefore follows that our sense of being an entirely separate self is little more than an illusion that obscures from us the real nature of our experience.[101].

It is this illusion that underlies our egotism, i.e., our self-importance, our aggression, and the various dimensions of our desire for material possessions or institutional (e.g., political) power. But the ultimate origin of egotism in itself is neither a moral failure nor a controversial political ideology. Rather, it is caused by a lack of understanding (of the interlocking conditions that bind us to others) and by the faulty emotional habits that follows from this lack of understanding. Equally, compassion should not be treated as deserving of special moral approval but as an obvious and necessary consequence of proper insight into who and what we are as human beings. Our *connectedness* with others is so essential to an understanding of what sort of 'beings' we are, that indifference or cruelty toward others is as irrational as self-harm, and 'generosity' towards others can be seen as simply the best way of looking after our own long-term interests.

Conversely, the need for compassion towards others is as self-evident as understanding that if we have an illness, we need to take our medication!

Perhaps this ethical implication seems surprising and challenging, but the underlying teaching, that individual phenomena are dependent on their conditions, was not only fundamental to Buddhism 2.500 years ago [102], but is also familiar as the first principle of modern 'systems theory': biologists know that an individual organism can only be fully understood in relation to its environment; environmentalists know that the fate of a species is dependent on the processes of its ecology; social workers know that the problems of a child or a parent must be understood in relation to the dynamics of the whole family; and social theorists interpret a given institution in terms of its functioning in society as a whole.

This same teaching ('conditionality' as the underlying basis for the ethics and politics of compassion) has equally profound consequences for the way we understand the scope of our responsibilities. Actions have consequences, but we can't know them all because they are innumerable: the processes of interconnectedness are, in principle, universal and never-ending; so that our knowledge of these connections is always incomplete (as well as, in the end, uncertain). But what *is* certain, in contrast, is that because of the connectedness of all events we can never deny *all* responsibility for the situations which surround us. ('No man is an island...') And neither can we circumscribe the timescale we are willing to consider as relevant (see Chapter Two on election intervals). The question is not, therefore, 'Do I bear any responsibility for the political ills of the world' (for racial injustice, for attacks on ambulance drivers, for homelessness, for climate degradation, etc.)? Instead, a better question would be: 'Given that I understand the element of responsibility for these things that, ultimately, I have to accept, can I think of a realistic, practical way in which I could respond?'

In various ways, then, the principles and practices of meditation challenge the way we think about our ethical responsibilities. And a comparable challenge is elaborated by Alasdair MacIntyre in his book *After Virtue: A Study in Moral Theory*. The starting point for his argument is that in modern (post-eighteenth century) society we have lost what he calls the 'classical' conception of human beings as bound together in societal processes of mutual obligation, i.e., embedded in a 'role', as 'a member of a family, citizen, soldier, etc...'. Instead, our contemporary self-understanding starts from the concept of 'an individual prior to and apart from all roles' [103]. Thus, our sense of our role obligations (e.g., our sense of how we ought to behave) has become separated from our sense that a human being's 'essential purpose' or essential 'nature' [104] arises from our connectedness with others (a central feature of the awareness arising from meditation, as previously noted). As a result, lacking this essential focus on our connectedness with our fellow human beings, MacIntyre argues, our current model of how we make collective decisions is based on nothing more than the arithmetic of individual expressions of 'preferences' [105]. In the ethical sphere, this means attempting to calculate 'What creates the greatest happiness for the greatest number'. But since the possible forms of human happiness are infinitely varied, they can never be compared or combined. So, any such calculation is 'interminable' because it 'has no clear sense'. Consequently, says MacIntyre, "There seems to be no rational way of securing moral agreement in our culture" [106].

To remedy this drastic absence at the heart of our current moral thinking, MacIntyre reminds us of Aristotle's theory of *'the virtues'*. 'Virtues', says MacIntyre, following Aristotle, may be thought of as qualities which express what is incontestably 'good' for human beings and human society [107]. And this returns us, precisely, to Aristotle's discussion of anger in Chapter One. For Aristotle, anger (in political life and in general) always needs to be controlled by *patience* – one of his lists of the moral and intellectual 'virtues', which also includes, for example, courage, truthfulness, friendship, wisdom and understanding [108].

For Aristotle a virtue is always a 'mean' or middle way between two extremes; for example, the virtue of 'courage' lies midway between 'cowardice' and 'and 'rashness', suggesting responsiveness to the detail of specific situations. This is similar to the emphasis in the Buddhist tradition, where the 'middle way' always represents a nuanced and subtle *awareness,* avoiding extreme polarised responses either of self-indulgence or self-denial [109]; which reminds us also of the focussed, concentrated awareness that is a key element in meditation practice. For MacIntyre the point about the Aristotelian conception of the virtues is that (unlike other human qualities, which we may admire, or not, as we choose, or depending on our cultural values), they are qualities that are always *incontestably* good. They don't express a type of personality or a point of view or a political ideology: they are intended to express what, in general it takes to be a human being, not in the abstract, as a separate individual, but *as a member of a community.* And not just a particular community, but *any* community.

And this is exactly the sort of claim that (I am arguing) could be made for the qualities, habits of awareness, and capacities that arise from the sustained practice of meditation. In other words, these qualities, capacities and habits of awareness are beneficial for us all – as citizens, irrespective of our membership of any particular faith, intellectual persuasion or political grouping.

A number of these 'meditation virtues', as we might call them, were described at the beginning of this chapter and listed in a more summarised form at the beginning of this section – i.e., the habitual practices of seeking to become:

more focused, more integrated, more objective, more honest (with oneself and others), more open-minded, more self-questioning, more appreciative, more comprehensive in our understanding, more imaginatively aware of the impermanence and interconnectedness of our experiences, more aware of our connectedness with others, more aware of the self-interested motives underlying so many of our impulses, and more aware of our inescapable responsibility for the consequences of our actions in the world.

To use the term 'virtues' to describe the outcomes we hope will arise from meditation may seem awkward; but the phrase I used earlier ('qualities, capacities and habits of awareness') is even more so, and at least 'virtues' is shorter! And although referring to 'virtues' may seem rather 'old fashioned', the term is familiar: we know intuitively what 'virtues' ought to be. 'Virtues' are habitual tendencies, acquired through practice, to act and think and feel in a way that is unquestionably beneficial *for any individual and for any community* [110] Insofar as these 'meditation virtues' have important political implications, as I have argued, we could also call them 'political virtues'. However, in spite of their undoubted political relevance, they are essentially based in psychological, intellectual and philosophical dimensions of our experience even though they are expressed of course as ethical or political values. And it is for this reason that we might hope they could gain general agreement, beyond ideological or party affiliation.

Perhaps we can go further and suggest that meditation practices indicate what is needed if we are *really* going to change – if we are genuinely to *learn* from our collective experience; so that the accumulated cultural wisdom of humanity doesn't just sit neatly classified on library shelves but is realised in our actual responses of care and compassion towards others. Otherwise, the current state of affairs will continue: the wisdom of our philosophical and spiritual classics is all available in paperback from any good bookshop – and meanwhile the world goes to hell in a handcart...

Alternatively, if meditation were to become established and widespread, we might finally become capable of *being the world we wish to see.* In which case meditation may prefigure not only a transformation of the moral order in which we participate as individuals, but also of the political order in which we participate as citizens.

******

Clearly, those last paragraphs were intended as the conclusion of my argument, and it might have been tempting to leave it there. But this is a book that is concerned to establish conditions for changing habits and behaviour; not just presenting arguments. Presenting arguments is fine, but it leads at best to libraries of wisdom, which some of us consult – with interest but also with dismay; as we contemplate the divergence, the discordance, between the world of ideas and the world in which we live with one-another. Yes, I have tried to make the argument convincing, but even more I have tried to make this a book for us all to *practise* with.

So, in many ways I think of the Practical Guide that follows as the most helpful part. It addresses questions like: "How long?" When? "Could chanting help?" and "Is it a good idea to open your eyes when you meditate?" I wrote it above all for myself, to keep by me as a set of reminders, but also for anyone and for everyone. If you are already an experienced meditator with a regular practice, you may not need the next section; so, feel free to stop reading now! (But you never know: meditation is such an 'inward' activity it is always interesting to have someone else's take on it.) But otherwise, please read on: this is where it gets not only interesting but even more important!

Chapter Five
A Practical Guide to
Meditation Methods

This is my very favourite Buddhist story. Someone taking part in a meditation course says to the teacher: "Somehow I don't seem to be able to get on with meditation; I find it so hard, I'm afraid I'm not really cut out for it." The teacher replies, "I see. And what makes you think *you* are so special?"

Meditation really is something we can *all* do. The question is: are we motivated to keep working at it? The first problem we may come across is finding time to fit it in alongside everything else in our busy lives – in other words: how to give it priority.

Which brings me to my other 'very favourite' Buddhist story: a man was chopping up logs into firewood. On one side of him was a small pile of firewood and on the other side of him was an enormous pile of logs. A passer-by watched him chopping away for a few minutes, making very slow progress, and concluded that the man's axe must be very blunt. So, he said to the woodchopper, "It looks to me as though that axe you are using is rather blunt; I think you might get on better if you got it sharpened." The woodchopper laughed. "You must be joking," he said. "Can't you see that great pile of logs I've got to chop up; how am I ever going to find time to sharpen my axe as well?" This really implies the theme of the whole book. Meditation, I am arguing, has a very practical purpose and this practical purpose is not just for ourselves (enabling us to feel a bit more OK in a difficult world) but for others: enabling us to become more *effective* in trying to make the world *less* difficult, for others as well as ourselves – which is where politics comes in. So, we don't need to worry that making time to meditate is somehow a 'self-indulgence'. Indeed, I am proposing that we shouldn't even think if it as any sort of 'optional extra'!

This 'Practical Guide' presents a variety of suggestions and observations based on my own experience of meditating, teaching meditation, reading, and studying over more than twenty years. Some readers, having experience of meditation, may find one or two of the details already familiar and even redundant. But my basic assumption is that many readers may not have tried meditation before, and so I have included all the practical detail I could think of that I have found useful in the past.

The chapter begins with suggestions on preliminary matters (such as where to meditate and for how long, etc.) and on issues concerning our meditation experience in general, such as typically encountered difficulties and the value of forming a support group. It would probably be helpful for those new to meditation to begin by reading the whole of this part of the chapter as a general introduction.

Later sections provide practical observations specifically focussing on different meditation processes, such as those introduced in Chapter Three. These later sections should be read one by one, alongside the relevant sections of Chapter Three, as a way of preparing for each of the meditation practices. It is also a good idea to re-read them several times until the sequence of steps for each practice has become familiar, because it is distracting to be wondering what comes next!

Where? (And Whether or Not to Close Our Eyes)

The initial advice in the early texts is to start by going to a forest or finding 'a deserted hut' [111]. However, neither forests nor deserted huts are always easy to find these days, so, more practically, the idea is to decide on a place that will help us to 'focus', free from distractions. It is a good idea to meditate regularly in a particular spot, which might be a specific room or a corner of a room, and it needs to be a place where we can remain undisturbed by other people's activities and where we can be fairly certain of this. Being able to concentrate is crucial, and we don't want to be distracted or to be worrying that we *might* be distracted. A further helpful idea is to place something in this space that can help our focussing: flowers, for example, or a candle, or a visual image that we find especially attractive or which has a special meaning for us. Something that will help us to feel positively about our meditation space but without distracting us with any strong associations.

On the other hand, noticing the traditional reference to a 'forest' and remembering that the early followers of the Buddha would usually have meditated outdoors [112], we might try meditating in the garden – if we are fortunate enough to have one. This can be quite inspiring – the sound of the wind, the variety of colours, the swaying of leaves, the varying light, the feel of nature's energy. We can appreciate all this even if we are meditating with our eyes closed. If we meditate with our eyes open, beware: enthusiastic gardeners may be distracted by noticing a bit of weeding or pruning that suddenly seems urgent.

Whether or not to close one's eyes is an interesting issue. Some people feel that it is somehow 'unnatural' to sit with one's eyes closed, especially when meditating in the company of others (see the section on 'The Value of a Support Group', below). But when our eyes are open, our attention is more easily caught by objects in our field of vision, which can set off a train of thought. This can be distracting; but not necessarily a major problem; because noticing that our attention has been distracted from the object of the meditation (e.g., the breath) and bringing it back again is a central part of the practice. Conversely, with our eyes closed we are more likely to start to feel drowsy, which *is* a major problem; and when this happens one immediate remedy is to open our eyes.

As a solution to the general question, it is often suggested that when we have our eyes open, we look at the floor a couple of metres ahead of us, but making sure that our eyes are only half-focussed.

How Long?

Ten minutes is OK to begin with, but it rather depends on the form of meditation. For 'Mindfulness of Breathing' ten

119

minutes allows time to focus fully on each of the four stages. For the 'Body Scan' also ten minutes is adequate. But for the 'Cultivating Kindness' meditation, for example, twenty minutes would be preferable, even at first. The important thing is not to rush or 'skip over' or 'just think about' any of the steps, but to give them sufficient time for the focussing effort of the meditation to succeed in slowing down the mind's activity, so as to create, in the end, a different state of mind or feeling.

However, as we become more practiced, we will probably find that we can usefully do a short breathing or body-scan meditation during the three or four minutes when we are waiting in a queue – in a shop, at traffic lights or on the telephone. In the end, after a few weeks of regular practice, thirty minutes may feel like a natural length of time – again depending on the form of our meditation.

At a certain point in the meditation there is often a sense that there has been a 'movement' in our state of being, a shift in our feelings, our mood, our understanding. And that's quite a good time to stop. It is not a good idea (i.e., it can be a distraction) to have a certain length of time as an aim. If we have an important engagement as our next activity after our meditation practice, it is a good idea to set a timer to ring a bell at least ten minutes or so beforehand, to make sure our attention is not distracted by a fear that our meditation may make us late for something.

When?

At first, it is easier to decide on a specific time of the day as a regular meditation time, especially if our lives are quite heavily scheduled. Early in the morning is frequently recommended, because it means that our minds have not already become burdened with our anxieties about the day's forthcoming events. In this way a meditation is a way of 'getting the day off to a good start'. Late at night is another suggestion, and in this case our meditation is an opportunity to *evaluate* the day (which can be helpful) and also a way of calming and focussing our thoughts and feelings as an effective preparation for sleep. (Not a good idea to try to meditate when we are already in bed, however, because this can encourage us to fall asleep *during* the meditation!) My own preference is for the early morning. But if the pattern of a particular day makes that inconvenient, I have often found that a late evening, pre-sleep meditation is also very effective.

On the other hand, it is important to be flexible. If we have a regular time set aside each day and then something unexpected turns up, we don't want to feel that we have 'missed' our meditation for today and simply postpone it till tomorrow: there might be another time when we actually *could* meditate later in the day. And also, something can occur that makes us want to meditate – even makes us feel that we *need* to meditate – and this can be at any point in the day. Indeed, although the benefits of an early morning meditation were recommended earlier, our underlying theme is politics; so, we can be open to the idea that a meditation can also be helpful as a way of responding to the morning's news!

'Posture'

Perhaps meditation exists in our minds as an image of someone sitting on a cushion with their legs crossed in the 'lotus' position. And we can feel bewildered and somewhat intimidated when a Zen teacher observes, mysteriously, *"To take this posture is itself to have the right state of mind."* 'How can 'posture' equate to a 'state of mind'?' we feel like asking. However, we can take heart when the same Zen teacher continues, "There is no need to obtain a special state of mind' and implies that it is just as essential to 'take the right posture when you are driving your car" [113] as when we meditate. So, we can choose to interpret his advice in a way that brings out its more practical implications.

For a start, cushions are *not* essential. We can obtain a 'meditation cushion' quite readily via the internet – a single one if we wish to meditate sitting with our legs crossed; or several, to make a small pile, if we wish to meditate kneeling astride them. But for most of us the most obvious meditation position is sitting on a chair. Not an armchair or an easy chair, but an ordinary straight-backed chair.

Whether we are using cushions or a chair, the 'right posture' for meditation, as for driving a car, is simply a position in which we feel comfortable. The essence of meditation is concentration, and not being comfortable is going to be a distraction that will prevent us from concentrating. Similarly, the 'right state of mind' is – to begin with – nothing 'special' but simply a sense of feeling physically comfortable and also a sense of well-being arising from *confidence* that we will be able to maintain this comfortable posture for an extended period of time. This follows directly from the two key characteristics of the meditation posture: we want to be at the same time *relaxed* and *alert;* for meditation practice we need a balance between tranquillity and energy.

In order to give ourselves the best chance of achieving this balance, the following suggestions are generally agreed:

- Imagine your head suspended from above, with your neck gently stretched so that your head feels 'light' on your shoulders. (Or imagine your head as a balloon filled with helium!)
- Tuck your chin in slightly, so that if you were to open your eyes you would be looking at the floor about two metres ahead of you.
- Relax your shoulders (i.e., sloping downwards and backwards).
- Make sure that your arms and hands don't feel heavy; so, support them, either in your lap (perhaps on a small cushion) or on your knees.
- Allow your spine to adopt its natural curve – neither slouched nor stiffly upright.
- Notice very carefully the angle that the base of your spine makes with your pelvis. It is easily adjusted by shifting around a bit. Make sure that you are not leaning forwards or backwards, and find the angle that feels most comfortable.
- When you have found the best angle for you, relax the muscles of your stomach and abdomen. It is OK to adjust this angle again during the meditation, if necessary.

- The tradition of sitting cross-legged on a cushion reminds us that it has been found, over the years, that it is better if our hips are slightly higher than our knees. On a chair this is achieved by placing a firm cushion on the seat of the chair – a wedge-shaped cushion is often helpful, or by raising the back legs of the chair on blocks of wood about three centimetres thick.

- Make sure that your weight is not only being supported by your buttocks on the chair but also in part by your feet on the floor; so that your sitting position is a sort of 'tripod' with a broad triangular base.

- Finally, don't be too focussed on the details: the main thing is to feel as comfortable as possible.

'Obstacles'[114]

In other words: things that 'get in the way' when we are trying to meditate. We might initially think of external conditions, such as lack of space, workers digging up the road with a pneumatic drill outside our window, unexpected visitors or phone calls, etc. But a more interesting problem is the way in which 'obstacles' originate in the state of our own thoughts and emotions. We may be feeling upset either by something that has just happened or by a sudden memory that has just re-surfaced. Consequently, we may recognise that we need first of all to just sit and notice the nature of our feelings and then perhaps do the 'Mindfulness of Breathing' meditation, described below, in order to collect and concentrate ourselves.

Traditional Buddhist teachings usually list five states of mind and feeling that constitute obstacles:

- We may find that our mind is feeling **Restless** – focussed on seeking new experiences: thoughts, memories, hopes, desires or fantasies;
- We may find that our mind is feeling **Negative** – responding with animosity, ill-will or envy to people, and with irritation to events and sensations;
- We may find that our mind is feeling **Anxious** – focusing on problems, fears, past errors, future dangers or guilt;
- We may find that our mind is feeling **Sluggish** – this may just be a matter of feeling physically tired, or it can be caused by boredom, apathy or depression.
- We may find that our mind is beset by **Doubt** – doubting ourselves (our worthiness), our ability to meditate, or whether meditation itself is worthwhile;

It is important to remember that these obstacles are not unusual or personal lapses on our part, but are to be expected, as the sort of thing that minds in general regularly get up to. This is what makes concentration so difficult. Indeed, in the traditional texts there are frequent comparisons between controlling the mind and taming an elephant. For example: "…if the elephant of the mind is completely restrained by the rope of mindfulness, then all perils vanish and complete well-being is obtained." [115]

Our response to an 'obstacle' should therefore always involve an element of acceptance. This might mean gently acknowledging the presence of the obstacle, while returning to a focus on the breath; or cultivating a sense of relaxed interest and even curiosity towards whatever is 'there' in our meditation. Other useful strategies are: remembering to hold any *expectations* of our meditation very lightly; and focusing with optimism on the basic principle that 'everything changes'. Finally, a frequent recommendation is that we should *visualise* whatever seems to be causing a problem *in a vast space, like the sky*, so that it can float away.

This last suggestion is also what is recommended when we are distracted by any thought or feeling that interrupts our focus during the course of our meditation. These may not really be 'obstacles' at all, but just helpful reminders of the need to concentrate: indeed, gently and repeatedly bringing our mind back to our focus is what the process of meditation largely consists of. And at best, such thoughts can sometimes actually bring helpful insights of one sort or another – see the section on 'The Unconscious' in Chapter Three.

Absorption and Enjoyment

One way or another, meditation is generally described as a process of 'concentration', or 'directing our attention' in a certain direction. This is fine, but it does sound rather austere, rather like hard work! So, it is useful to consider the implications of another word, *'absorption'*, which is also frequently used in this context – i.e., to differentiate our 'ordinary' state of mind from our state of mind during meditation practice. And when we think about what it is like to be 'absorbed' in something, a central aspect of the experience, we would probably agree, is that *enjoyment* plays a large part. What activity, for example, do we typically enjoy so much that we get 'absorbed'? It's worth thinking of examples here. From my own experience: reading, listening to music, playing the piano. Other people's examples, when I posed the question, included swimming, gardening, water-colour painting, and cycling; and I know my father would have said: working on his stamp collection! What do these have in common? Losing track of time, perhaps; because we are so wrapped up in what we are doing that it involves every bit of our attention. And a strong sense of enjoyment is part of it too.

Thus, we want to be able to approach our meditation practice, *not simply as a task but as a pleasure.* In an early text, the Buddha describes the state of being absorbed in meditation as containing not just 'thought and examination' but 'rapture and happiness'. And as we get even more absorbed, our mind becomes less analytical and more effortlessly integrated, and 'rapture and happiness' continue to be part of our experience [116]. Some interpretations of the traditional teachings make absorption seem part of a difficult process, but others emphasise that this need not be so [117]. So, I take comfort and guidance from the expectation that my meditation practice will probably be more like walking through a beautiful landscape than vacuuming the stairs!

This throws light on the familiar emphasis that meditation as a *practice* has something in common with practising a musical instrument or a sport. In both cases there is training that involves both endless repetition and the minute detail of a technique. How many times did we re-play that passage until we thought it sounded really good? How many lengths of the swimming pool did we swim until the water felt as though it was just slipping past us with no effort? And what about the amazing performances of those who go in for skating or gymnastics? Why do we/they do it? It's not about competing (although unfortunately our culture tries to make *everything* into a competition, no matter how inappropriate). It is simply about that sense of well-being that arises from our enjoyment of being able to do something difficult with ease and grace.

My point is that there is nothing unusual about this aspect of meditation (i.e., the combination of repetition and enjoyment) because the analogy is broader even than developing an artistic or sporting ability. It is an essential aspect of all *real* learning, i.e., learning to do something out of our own motivation, because what we are trying to learn seems so worthwhile and important in itself that we become absorbed in what we are engaged in and *enjoy* the repetition.

Rituals, 'Mantras'

The idea of being absorbed in an activity that is frequently *repeated* is a reminder that the cultural traditions underlying meditation practice often place an emphasis on *ritual* activity. Many of us may feel rather worried by this, since our contemporary culture tends to pride itself on spontaneity and individualism, which at first seem to stand opposed to what we think of as ritual. However, meditation entails a critique of *self*-orientation, as noted at many points in the argument so far, and an emphasis, instead, on connectedness with others.

And we also want to *feel* different and somehow to *be* different. So, it is helpful to have at least some way of 'getting started' in our effort to enter a different frame of mind, and we could think of this as a form of ritual, simply as a way of 'welcoming' ourselves to our meditation. A minimal 'welcome' would be, for example, three deep breaths. Or we could light a candle.

Or we could recite a 'mantra'. A mantra can be any phrase that has significance for us, one we have grown up with or one that we have made up or adapted, which refers in some way to our *purpose* in meditating and which has a nice rhythm to it, so that it is enjoyable to recite it three times (or so). "Freedom, Justice, and Equality" might work, or, what about "Generosity, Truth, and Compassion"? Make one up and see if it works for you! If necessary, keep experimenting. Over the years, the phrase I have come to use is: 'May I not cause harm to other beings.' I like both its rhythm and its ambiguity (What, in different situations, would be 'harm'?), so it makes me feel good just to say it. In a way its function is rather like saying to myself, 'Good morning, nice to be here, meditating!' Although the word 'mantra' now has the popular meaning of a phrase that is repeated as a ritual, in the original Sanskrit, the term meant 'an *instrument* of thought' [118], so it seems quite appropriate to suggest that reciting a mantra can have a practical purpose.

Resources: A Support Group, CDs, Books

Although we practice meditation individually, there is no doubt that the mutual support provided by a group of likeminded friends can be invaluable. We don't need, or even want, a large group. Four or five would be a maximum number and just two would be enough. The advantage of a small group is that it is easier for each of us to take turns in *sharing* our meditation experiences.

And 'likeminded' is important, because we need to ensure that we are all really serious about our meditation 'project'; and, most importantly of all, are prepared to talk openly about our own thoughts and feelings and to listen carefully to everyone else's. This, like so much else, is easier said than done, and these 'support conversations' are likely to present some of the same issues as meditation itself, e.g., fully sympathising with each other's experience and not insisting on our own point of view. At first, we might feel that this sort of conversation would probably not be interesting to quite a lot of the people we know. But there again, we may find that in the present climate meditation is widely familiar and not at all controversial. And anyway, it only takes two people to start a group!

I have found that sessions involving meditation and discussion of our meditation experience can also work quite well online, i.e., using 'Zoom' technology. This of course expands our range of possible partners, and makes it easier to arrange 'meetings'.

Another readily available source of support is the range of websites where we can find advice and explanations on meditation in general, and CDs with 'guided meditations' which will go step-by-step through the different stages of some of the meditations. However, websites teachers are inevitably different from each other, and all of them (probably) will differ in some ways from the particular emphasis in this book. At first this variety of material may not always feel very helpful, but there is of course no single 'correct' way to meditate, and it is always useful to compare and experiment with contrasting approaches.

Finally, here are some books that I have repeatedly found helpful and would strongly recommend – clearly written, convincing and accessible:

Parmananda *Change Your Mind – A Practical Guide to Meditation,* Windhorse Publications, 1996

Vessantara: *The Art of Meditation – The Breath,*
Windhorse Publications, 2005

Vessantara: *The Art of Meditation – The Heart,*
Windhorse Publications, 2006

The 'Body Scan'

This is the most immediate specific form of practice, and can be a meditation practice on its own. It is also very often used as a preliminary exercise before moving on to another form of meditation. It involves moving the focus of our awareness to a different area of the body in turn, noticing the various sensations and creating a series of intense but momentary points of concentration. It is tempting to try to combine a 'body scan' with setting up our posture, but I find this doesn't work very well because a different sort of attention is required.

One issue is simply how long to spend on it. Too long and it becomes tedious and we lose concentration; too short and we find our attention just 'sliding over' the body; so that we don't really experience a sense of our attention being 'arrested' in a way that differs from our usual experience of our body as something that we take more or less for granted. Also, the sensations in one part of the body may be particularly intense, so that we naturally want to spend rather longer concentrating on it. In order to break out of our 'routine' body awareness, it can be helpful to be conscious of using the *breath* in order to *carry* our attention. Thus, we might take three or four breaths as we focus on one area of our body after another – noticing and accepting whatever we experience there, without attempting to change it. And if we are experiencing a lot of pain, we may consciously send our breath to that part of our body to acknowledge and 'greet' the pain.

Our bodies contain very many different 'subdivisions'; so, which are we going to select for our scan? It would be tedious and distracting to try to notice *all* of them; instead, it is helpful to start by noticing which parts of our body arise spontaneously in our awareness. At first, perhaps, sensations of the face (mouth, ears, nose, and eyes); then, for many of us, our joints and our muscles, each with their array of intermittent aches; for others the sensations of the stomach are always potentially interesting. Our aim is always *just to notice and accept.* The body-scan meditation is a process of 'becoming mindful of', 'really getting to know', or 'making friends with' our individual body. So rather than working systematically through all the 'components' of bodies in general, let us allow our particular body to suggest to us (on the occasion of *this* meditation: *next* time it may well be different) what is of interest, in what way, and for how long.

'The Mindfulness of Breathing'

The reason why breathing is (and has been) so universally accepted as the basis of meditation practice is not merely that we depend on it to stay alive, but because it is our most accessible aid to concentration. The Buddha is reported to have practised the 'Mindfulness of Breathing' meditation regularly, and to have recommended breathing meditation for *everyone*, no matter how advanced their spiritual practice; because "it leads to a pleasant dwelling in this very life and to mindfulness and clear comprehension." [119]

It is also helpful to incorporate our breathing, one way or another, into *all* our meditation practices. In this way we can *feel* the breath focusing our awareness in a particular direction during the different stages of the meditation, and this ensures that our efforts of concentration are differentiated from 'merely thinking'. This process was referred to in the previous section on 'The Body Scan'. It is also a crucial aspect of an ancient Tibetan teaching, where we 'send out' our compassion to ease the sufferings of others. In order to do so we imagine our compassion 'riding the breath' – the traditional phrase vividly evoking the experience of using our breath to express our *wishing well* in a way that is 'heart-felt', rather than merely 'a thought in the mind'.

There are four stages to the Mindfulness of Breathing practice itself.

The first two stages involve *counting* the breaths.

In stage one, we count each breath *after the out-breath*, and then make a short pause before beginning the next breath. So, the pattern is:

- Breathe in; breathe out, count 'one'; pause; breathe in; breathe out; count 'two'; pause and so on, up to 'ten'.
- After counting to ten we start again at one, and if we lose count for any reason, we start again at one.

In stage two, we count *before the in-breath*. The pattern now is:

- Count 'one'; breathe in; breathe out; pause; count 'two'; breathe in; breathe out; pause; count 'three', and so on up to 'ten'.
- Again, after counting to ten we start again at one, and if we lose count for any reason, we start again at one.

The shift of rhythm between stage one and stage two, is quite tricky, and for that reason is a further aid to concentration. In order to manage the shift of rhythm I find I need to take a couple of 'blank' breaths, i.e., without counting, between the two stages.

- We are not trying to breathe in a particular way (short or long, deep or shallow) but simply to 'observe' each breath as it arises. This is the reason for the pause: it helps us allow each breath to be different and gives us space to notice the difference in the rhythm. In stage one we are conscious that the breath has now

134

become a moment in the past, and in stage two we are conscious of the breath as a moment that is about to occur.

In stage three, we no longer count: instead we notice intensely the two phases of the breath.

- On the in-breath we enjoy as fully as we can the experience of our thoughts and feelings being 'integrated' – a sense of collectedness, consolidation, 'togetherness', and strength.
- On the out-breath we enjoy as fully as we can the experience of 'letting go' – a sense of relaxation, acceptance and tranquillity.
- In the alternation between the two we can actually *feel* the principle of 'impermanence' in action, as each breath is succeeded by the next, and as we 'let go' (on the out-breath) what we have 'collected together' (on the in-breath).
- We can also enjoy the slow alternation to and fro between the two phases as a source of purely physical pleasure. The breath *calms* the body and the body *calms* the breath, in a gentle rocking motion. Personally, I experience this as though my body has become like a small boat rising and falling on the waves at the edge of the sea. For others the effect may be something like swimming or riding a horse.

<u>In stage four</u>, we focus on the breath as a single moment.

- Previously, we have focused on the breath as an extended process that we watch in detail, as it enters our mouth and progresses down through our throat and lungs, expands our diaphragm, and then moves back up again and finally is exhaled. Now, in stage four, we just concentrate on that single moment when the breath enters the mouth or the nose, which we can experience as a 'puff' of relatively cold air.

- This is a particularly intense way of experiencing *concentration,* and in that sense is the climax of the meditation. In order to fully experience that puff of cold air we need to allow the breath to become very gentle, almost imperceptible. There is a danger that at this point we start to breathe very short, and this can feel hurried. So instead, we have to breathe in very gently, and also to allow the rest of the breath to 'tail away' equally gently, almost without our attention, while we prepare for the next 'puff' of the in-breath. When we do manage this process of 'reducing' the breath, the concentration effect is very powerful.

Impulses and Emotions:
'Finding the Gap'

This form of practice plays an important part in each of the following meditation sequences. The teaching on which it is based arises from the Pali term *vedana.* This can be translated either as 'sensation' or as 'feeling'; but in English, of course (although *not* in Pali) a 'feeling' can be not only a momentary impulse (as in *vedana*) but also an extended experience, i.e., an 'emotion'. The substance of the teaching is that every experience of a sustained state of emotion (e.g., anger, delight, fear, irritation, jealousy, sorrow, etc, etc.) always starts off as a momentary impulse (*vedana*) which is either positive, negative, or neutral [120].

Any experience that engages our feelings or which has any sort of ethical significance presents us, therefore, with an interesting opportunity. It presents us with a tiny temporal *gap* between the initial 'stimulus' (a sound, a sight, or what someone has just said, or a sudden bodily pain, etc) and our reaction to that stimulus. And it is in this 'gap' that we can find the possibility of *delaying*, just by an instant, our immediate but possibly unhelpful reaction, and of finding instead a response that is more sensitively adapted to the situation. This is the basic process whereby we are able to 'detach' ourselves from spontaneous impulses of egotism (greed, self-importance, indifference, or animosity) and instead recollect (and act on) the values underlying our meditation practice. It is this possibility that is being referred to when the Buddha is reported as saying, "Just as the great ocean has one taste, the taste of salt, so also [what the Buddha teaches] has one taste, the taste of liberation." [121] We have the possibility, in other words, of *freeing* ourselves from our immediate impulses and reaching a better understanding of, and a more helpful response to our experience. And this, precisely, is the basis for the optimism concerning our capacity for change that underlies meditation practice.

Opportunities to improve a situation by 'finding the gap' are of course not limited to those we encounter when meditating on a chair: on the contrary, it is a practice that we can easily take out into the rest of our lives. It is quite illuminating to start to list all those situations where we regularly have unhelpful impulses that are guaranteed to be counterproductive, both by making ourselves feel even worse than before, or by generating further antagonism in someone else. For example: stuck behind someone who cannot find their credit card in a supermarket queue when we are in a hurry; someone driving a lorry much too close behind us; someone driving a car much too slowly ahead of us; someone at an adjacent table in a restaurant talking too loudly in a pompous/squeaky voice; in a meeting, when someone we disagree with does not understand the very simple point we are trying to make; in the same meeting, when someone we agree with completely fails to make our point of view sound convincing. Please continue for yourself; I can hardly bear to stop! The point is that many moments of our lives are opportunities for 'liberation' from our unhelpful initial responses to events by 'finding the gap' in the moment before we react.

'Cultivating Metta'

The joy of the 'Mindfulness of Breathing' practice is the sense that our thoughts and emotions begin to feel less 'scattered', less restless, and thus more concentrated, more tranquil. At the end of a 'Cultivating *Metta*' meditation, the sensation is not dissimilar, but the emphasis is on feeling more 'connected', more confident, more 'at one with' our fellow beings.

But perhaps even to assert this difference of emphasis is to make a distinction where none is really necessary.

Although the main 'process' of cultivating *metta* is a sequence of visualisations, the images we visualise are more vivid and more deeply felt when we embody each one in our breathing, so that they 'ride our breath', to use the evocative Tibetan phrase quoted earlier. And in both meditations, there is an important element of *kindly acceptance* of whatever we find in our thoughts and feelings, as the stages of the practice unfold. For example, in 'The Mindfulness of Breathing' we may find that concentration is precisely what doesn't happen; and in the 'Cultivating *Metta*' practice we may find that when we contemplate ourselves and visualise others, we experience anger, envy or remorse, rather than the confidence or compassion we seek. And when this happens, we need to remember that such experiences are not our personal failures but general reminders of the complexity of meditation and the mysteriousness of our thoughts and feelings.

There are five stages to the practice.

<u>In Stage One</u>, we try to cultivate positive qualities in *ourselves,* such as, for example, kindness, generosity, sensitivity, so that we can *appreciate* ourselves as, let us say, open-minded and openhearted.

'If only!' I hear you cry, and I fully sympathise! Our feelings about ourselves are long-established habits, and habits are notoriously difficult to change. Many people, including experienced meditators, find this the most difficult section of the practice, and it is OK to experiment by starting at Stage Two, for example, and returning to Stage One later.

Nevertheless, let us not give up so easily: starting from a state of mind at the beginning of our meditation in which we actually feel rather blank or a bit negative, what can we do?

- Take several breaths, and really enjoy the sense of well-being that arises.
- Bring to mind, as vividly as we can, a time when we were really absorbed in a favourite activity.
- Remember a time when we felt 'uplifted' by an experience – perhaps a walk through a beautiful landscape or a beautiful part of a city, or listening to a favourite piece of music, or observing the zest and trustfulness of little children, or the sense of connectedness arising from a really good conversation – a sense of fully understanding and of being fully understood.
- Remember an occasion just recently when we *very nearly* said or did something (no matter how minor) that we know would have been a mistake; and instead, just in time, we spotted the problem and said or did something much more helpful, so that we can, in retrospect, enjoy and appreciate our sensitivity and thoughtfulness!
- Direct our awareness to a sense of confidence in the effectiveness of our meditation practice.
- Repeat our mantra three of four times (see earlier section). If you haven't yet decided on one, the following is often recommended: "*May I be well.*"

Stage Two, is usually less difficult. We bring to mind our feelings of affection and appreciation for a very good friend – preferably a friend who is roughly our age and for whom we have no romantic or sexual feelings (which can complicate matters).

- We start by bringing our friend to mind as vividly as we can, remembering details of her/his voice, gestures and way of walking.
- Remembering a recent occasion when we had an enjoyable meeting, trying to recall her/his clothes, and what we talked about.
- Thinking of particular qualities we appreciate in our friend – not listing them in words but trying to re-experience the different feelings they evoke in us.
- Sending our wishes for our friend's well-being to them, considering what would be the most appropriate 'mantra' for her/him. Perhaps simply 'May you be well'; or alternatively we may have a clear idea from our knowledge of her/him what sort of wish would be most welcome.
- *Breathing* our good wishes for our friend deep down into our heart.
- If we are aware that our friend is experiencing a significant level of suffering, sending out our *compassion* with our breathing, along with our good wishes.
- It is useful to check whether, mixed with our empathy ('sympathetic joy') for our friend's happiness and success, there is not a slight trace of envy. If so, we can try to let it go, by *breathing* it far way, out into the clear blue sky where we send our most unwelcome thoughts.

In Stage Three, we visualise someone whose face is familiar to us but who is otherwise a 'stranger' – the person who delivers our post or newspapers, perhaps, or a neighbour who frequently walks past our house but with whom we have not established any sort of relationship.

- For us the details of this person's life are initially a blank, so we have to start by *imagining* them: their relationships, their interests, their hopes and their anxieties.
- There may be something about the person that gives us some clues, but basically, we can start from the assumption that this 'familiar stranger' has the same sort of concerns as ourselves – friendships, family, illness, bereavement, financial security, and so on. So, as we imagine the various aspects of this person's life, we try to extend to them (with our breath making the connection) a sense of 'fellowship', a shared humanity, a sense that if we actually knew them, we might quite probably find that our lives are in many respects similar.
- Combining our breathing with imagining our common humanity with a stranger can give quite a powerful emotional charge to this stage of the practice.

Stage Four, can cause problems, since the basic idea is to try to feel more positively towards a 'difficult person' for whom we currently feel some degree of animosity or irritation: perhaps our interactions with her/him leave us feeling bruised, badly treated, and even angry. Our friends, family, colleagues, and neighbours may not at first seem to include obvious candidates for this role – but there will always be one or two, even if at first, we have to think hard to bring someone to mind.

- We start by allowing ourselves to stay with this feeling. It is OK to feel like this: our experiences of being badly treated by this person are as real as any of our other experiences.
- We then move on to imagine this person behaving in a quite different manner (humorous, sensitive, and tolerant) when involved in other relationships, with grandchildren, or caring for elderly relatives, or with close childhood friends, for example.
- Imagining difficult circumstances in this person's life with which we could sympathise – e.g., illness, disappointment, bereavement, so that instead of allowing our negative emotions to get 'hooked' we can begin to see a possibility for compassion.
- Perhaps we notice that what irritates us in this person is something in ourselves that, on reflection, we would like to change!
- The main thing, again, is to focus on our shared humanity with this person – our shared hopes and our shared fears; and with our breath send them our good wishes, wishing them well – 'in spite of everything'.

In Stage Five, we begin by imagining ourselves, our friend, our 'familiar stranger', and our 'difficult person' as joined together in a sense of kindliness that includes us all equally. We then try to expand the circle of our sympathetic awareness and understanding to include *anyone who comes to mind.* In other words: people who have made some sort of impression on us – perhaps we have met them in the street, or a shopping centre, or read about in the newspaper or seen on TV or social media. This is the stage where we put into practice the 'universal' dimension of the *'Metta Sutta'* (see Chapter Three, section v). So, we try to experience a sense of shared humanity with harassed parents, zestful toddlers, victims of disasters or wars, and even with the politicians and soldiers responsible for suffering.

This latter example is perhaps the most difficult challenge of all for the 'Cultivating *Metta'* meditation practice, and we should remember to feel compassion for ourselves when we contemplate our relative helplessness in the face of the world's political woes. However, Mary Trump's biography of her uncle Donald, the American president (reviewed in *The Guardian[G2],* July 23rd, 2020) offers an unexpected indication of how we can use our imagination to extend a sort of sympathy even to the most contentious of politicians. She describes how Trump's father publicly bullied, humiliated and marginalised Donald's elder brother, in order to terrorise the youthful Donald into behaving in the brutal way his father required of the son he wished to carry on his business empire. Thus, we can imagine how even our severest condemnation is compatible with understanding the suffering underlying the actions we are inclined to condemn.

So, armed with this understanding, perhaps we can see our possible responses in terms of seeking comprehensiveness and balance, rather than in terms of either despair or animosity. In other words, we try to respond in a way that is 'all-embracing' – summoning *all* our emotional and intellectual resources. We might sum up the whole argument by saying that our imagination challenges us to ask ourselves: "Is there anything *else* relevant here – anything that I am overlooking?"

Walking Meditation: Noticing Our Bodies, Noticing the World

"Lower back pain? I see. How many hours a day do you spend in front of a computer?" I remember very clearly the osteopath going on to say to me, rather tartly: "The human body is much better adapted to walking about than sitting in a chair." Walking meditation is not only the sort of meditation practice that an osteopath might recommend, but is also an enjoyable way of combining the practices of bodily awareness, breathing, and cultivating *metta*. And it is also another way of moving our meditation from our chair out into our lives generally, which is, of course, where we most need it. Any walk can become a meditation if we shift our main attention from the goal (getting somewhere) to the process of walking itself.

We start by focussing fully on our physical sensations, and this is not difficult, because the body in motion is in many ways an even more interesting subject for our close attention than the body at rest, as in 'The Body Scan' (see earlier section).

- Nevertheless, we start by standing still, noticing carefully the sensations in our feet, knees, hips, back, shoulders and arms; and in particular how the stability of our base depends on the forces of gravity to maintaining our balance.

- Then we begin to walk, just a little bit slower than normal; noticing the *interesting* sensations in our various joints and muscles, moving our attention between them, and noticing also the regular overall movement of our body and the rhythm of our weight shifting forwards and sideways.

- Gradually we coordinate the rhythm of our body's movement with the parallel rhythm of our breathing, by finding a pattern (i.e., the number of steps for each breath) that feels comfortable for us.

- We need to keep our main attention on the continuously varying sensations in our body as it moves, with the breath just as a background. The balance between these two elements of our experience provides us with a continuous focus for our concentration and a way of minimising distractions.

Distractions are of course an issue, since we have our eyes open even though our effort is to concentrate on our 'internal' experience; and this brings us to the second aspect of Walking Meditation, namely the link with 'Cultivating *Metta*'.

- While we are walking, the outside world passes before us. And so, walking meditation can present us with precise opportunities to develop our practice of cultivating *metta* without needing to visualise a series of people.

- First of all, we can develop *metta* by allowing ourselves to appreciate elements of beauty in trees and flowers (subtle shapes and colours) and in buildings (variety of detail, mixture of styles, etc). This can create a sense of spaciousness and delight that affects our whole being.

- Secondly, we can develop *metta* towards the various strangers who cross our path. We can try to be fully aware of them (their appearance, their demeanour, etc), in order to cultivate a positive response within ourselves towards them, acknowledging their full *presence* in our experience and our common humanity with them.

- However, becoming more fully aware of the people we notice will take a different form depending on the nature of our initial response. For example, we may experience an expansive sensation of delight towards a zestful toddler, whereas feelings of irritation or fear may be provoked by a group of shouting teenagers. These immediate reactions will often be based on stereotypes derived from spontaneous impulses that we will need to check and 'interrupt' (see section on 'Finding the Gap' above).

- Whenever we are led to notice things in the external world (e.g., trees, buildings or people) during our walking meditation, it can lead to distracting trains of thoughts (for example, when we are reminded of other similar experiences). When this occurs, we need to return to our focus on the detailed *physical movements of the body,* with which we started.

Although walking meditation can be extremely enjoyable, it is complex and takes an effort of concentration that can become quite difficult to sustain. So, if your walking meditation practice is part of a longer walk, it is a good idea to alternate walking meditation with periods of 'ordinary' walking.

*****

In some ways, I am pleased to end with this emphasis that although meditation starts with the simplest of actions it can end with the deepest of understandings and the subtlest of feelings. But for people fairly new to meditation it might seem a bit over-complicated. So, I'd like to end by returning briefly to some earlier points.

First: the remarkable effectiveness of just noticing our *breathing*. I remember so clearly the first time I took part in a meditation class, even though it was many years ago: I just could not believe that something so apparently simple as concentrating on my breathing could have such a dramatic effect on my mood. I say 'mood' because to call it my 'state of mind' is to leave out (as usual) *feelings*. And meditation always includes, of course, both. After fifteen minutes of 'watching my breath', I was both more relaxed and more alert, more 'at one with' myself and with the other people in the room.

Second: it is important to *enjoy* the meditations separately, one by one and also step by step: we don't always have to complete a sequence right to the end, although it is important to start at the beginning. We just need to be guided by how we feel; getting used to one meditation, or one stage of a meditation first, so that it starts to feel 'natural', before moving on.

This leads on to the importance of developing a *habit* of meditation through regular *practice.* The power of meditation arises most strongly when we practise it regularly so that it becomes a habit that affects the way we respond to life generally, at first in quite small ways but then on a larger scale. Our friends and family are often the first to notice.

Practice involves repetition of course, and after a while that can threaten to interfere with enjoyment. And that is why this Practical Guide contains a number of different meditations, precisely so that the variety of methods enables us to keep enjoying our meditation experience by *refreshing* it. Indeed, this was the reason why I became very interested in another traditional approach to meditation. It is based on a series of 'slogans' (fifty-nine of them altogether) which create an enjoyable variety to our practice just by giving us a different theme for the next day's meditation (described in my book *Don't Expect a Standing Ovation,* published in 2020 by Austin Macauley).

Practice and Variety! Treat the Guide as a reference, or perhaps as we might treat a book of recipes. We don't try to cook all the dishes at once! And neither do we really want to cook the same dish every day!

Endnotes

[1] Otto von Bismark, generally credited with having managed to achieve the unification of the German state.

[2] Sangharakshita: *Vision and Transformation,* Windhorse, 1999, p.30

[3] Daniel Goleman: *Emotional Intelligence: Why it can matter more than IQ,* Bloomsbury, 1996, p. xii;

[4] Daniel Goleman: op. cit., p. xiv

[5] Daniel Goleman: op. cit., p.xiv

[6] *The Guardian, April 3rd, 2020, p. 28*

[7] Daniel Goleman: op.cit., p. xiii

[8] Humphrey Hawksley: *Democracy Kills,* Macmillan, 2009

[9] Tony Benn: *The Best of Benn,* Hutchinson, 2014, p.241

[10] See Stephen Batchelor: *Buddhism Without Beliefs,* Bloomsbury, 1997

[11] Check the internet entries under 'mindfulness-based stress reduction'.

[12] Bikkhu Nanamoli: *The Life of the Buddha,* Buddhist Publication Society, 1992, pp.13–21

[13] Stephen Batchelor: op.cit., p. 4

[14] See for example the *Agganna Sutta,* in Maurice Walshe (trans.): *The Long Discourses of the Buddha,* Wisdom Publications, 1995, pp. 407-415;

Trevor Ling: *The Buddha,* Penguin, 1976, pp. 142

[15] There is indeed a politically active 'Network of Engaged Buddhists'. See for example, Ken Jones: *What is Engaged Buddhism?,* Pilgrim Press, 2012;

David Loy: *Money, Sex, War, Karma,* Wisdom Publication, 2008

[16] Vishvapani Blomfield: *Gautama Buddha: The Life and Teachings of The Awakened One,* Quercus, 2012, p. 216

[17] Peter Roman: *People's Power – Cuba's Experience with Representative Government,* Rowan and Littlefield, 2003; see especially pp. 85–6

[18] Caroline Lucas: *Honourable Friends?,* Portobello, 2015, p. 148

[19] Robert Michels: *Political Parties,* Dover Publications, 1959 [first published in 1915]

[20] This more general argument was elaborated in the 1970s by Talcott Parsons in his book *The Social System,* Routledge, 1970

[21] Yuval Harari: *Sapiens: A Brief History of Humankind,* Vintage, 2015, p. 51; p. 87

[22] Harari: op. cit., chapter 7

[23] *Forbes Magazine,* January 11th, 2019. See also 'Political Trust in the UK', *Full Fact,* June, 2019

[24] Onora O'Neill: *A Question of Trust,* Cambridge University Press, 2002, Preface, p.vii

[25] Confucius: *The Analects, XII,* 7, Penguin, 1979, p.113

[26] Richard Wilkinson & Kate Picket: *The Spirit Level*, Alan Lane, 2009, p.45; pp.52–3

[27] 'United Nations News, January 21st, 2020: 'Inequality is growing for more than 70% of global population'.

[28] Justice of the UK Supreme Court Lord Hodge: Lecture at Shanghai Jiao Tong University, Shanghai, October 24th 2018.

[29] Jean-Jacques Rousseau: *The Social Contract,* Oxford, 1994 [1762], pp.139–140

[30] David Van Reybrouck: *Against Elections*, Bodley Head, 2013

[31] Katie Allen, *The Guardian,* March 22, 2017

[32] See www.adamsmith.org/abouttheasi

[33] Paul Samuelson: *Economics,* International Student Edition, McGraw-Hill, 1980, p.784

[34] Paul Samuelson: op. cit., p. 785

[35] The richest 1% of the world's population own 44% of the world's wealth (Credit Suisse Global Wealth Report, 2019

[36] Adam Smith: *The Theory f Moral Sentiments,* Penguin, 2009, p.13

[37] Adam Smith: *The Wealth of Nations,* Penguin, 1970; pp. 169–70; p.232; p.359.

[38] Adam Smith: *The Theory of Moral Sentiments,* p.215

[39] Adam Smith: op.cit. pp. 278–9

[40] Robert Crumpton, 'Why do politicians lie?', *The Times,* December 6th, 2019

[41] USA National Security Council Directive NSC 5412/2 (undated)

[42] Machiavelli: *The Prince,* Penguin, 1962, p. 100

[43] See www.speakingtruthtopower.org

[44] Ibid.

[45] The Book of Genesis, chapter 4, verse 9.

[46] See www.wikipedia.org/wiki/Responsible_government

[47] Paul Samuelson: op.cit. p.785

[48] John Donne: *Devotions upon Emergent Occasions,* Meditation XVII

[49] Polly Toynbee and David Walker: 'Meet the Rich', *The Guardian,* August 4th, 2008

[50] See, for example:

P. A. Payutto: *Buddhist Solutions for the Twenty-first Century,* Buddhadhamma Foundation, 1994

P. A. Payutto: *Buddhist Economics,* Buddhadhamma Foundation, 1994

David Loy: *Money, Sex, War, Karma,* Wisdom Publications, 2008

John Stanley et al (Eds.): *A Buddhist Response to the Climate Emergency,* Wisdom Publications, 2009

Vaddhaka Linn: *The Buddha on Wall Street,* Windhorse, 2015

[51] See www.patheos.com/blogs/sermon from the mound/2014/95

[52] See Che Guevara: 'Socialism and Man in Cuba' [1965], in *The Che Reader,* Ocean Press, 2005

[53] Dating back to the 5th century text by the Buddhist commentator Buddhaghosa: *The Path of Purification,* (Translated by Bhikkhu Nanamloli), Buddhist Publication Society, 1991, Chapter VIII, verse 189

[54] In the original language (Pali): *The Anapanasati Teaching*

[55] Thich Nhat Hanh: *Breathe! You Are Alive,* Rider, 1992, p.8

[56] The *'Satipatthana'* Teaching

57 'Bahiya', in *The Udana & The Itivuttaka,* Buddhist Publication Society, 1997, pp. 19–21

58 Bhikkhu Bodhi: 'What does mindfulness really mean? A canonical perspective', in *Contemporary Buddhism,* Vol. 12 (i), 2011, p.26; p.27

59 Rupert Ghetin: 'On some definitions of mindfulness', in *Contemporary Buddhism,* Vol. 12 (i), 2011, p. 267

60 Especially when we note that the Buddha continued his teaching by advising Bahiya to experience, 'in the cognised...merely the cognised'. This seems like saying, 'When a thought occurs to you, don't think about it!' Which seems even more difficult!

61 See Martine and Stephen Batchelor: *What is this?,* Tuwhiri, 2019, p.11; p. 21; p.29

62 Bhikkhu Bodhi: op. cit., p.23; p.24; p.26

63 Bhikkhu Bodhi:op.cit., p.21; p.25

64 Sharon Salzberg: 'Mindfulness and Loving-Kindness', in *Contemporary Buddhism,* Vol. 12 (i), 2011, p. 178

65 *'Metta Sutta'* in *The Sutta-Nipata ,* Routledge Curzon, 1994, p. 16

66 Buddhaghosa: op. cit., pp. 288–290

67 Alternatively, the final stage of the meditation is often presented as the extension of our feeling of Loving-kindness to *all* living beings, imagined as expanding outwards geographically in a series of concentric circles.

68 The original (Pali) term for an 'impulse' of feeling is *'vedana'.* See Sangharakshita: *A Guide to the Buddhist Path,* 2nd Edition, Windhorse, 1996, pp.83–7

[69] Thich Nhat Hanh: *The Miracle of Mindfulness,* Rider, 2008, pp.130–1

[70] Percy Bysshe Shelley: 'A Defence of Poetry' (1821) in Raman Selden, Ed: *The Theory of Criticism – A Reader,* Longman, 1988, p. 484. [Slightly amended: i.e., 'humanity' and 'human beings' substituted for 'man'.]

[71] 'Kisa-Gotami', in *Poems of Early Buddhist Nuns,* (revised version), The Pali Text Society, 1989, pp.88–9

[72] In the original Pali the different forms of *metta* are called the *'Brahma-Viharas'.* See Sangharakshita: op.cit, pp. 159–63

[73] *Analayo: Satipatthana,; The Direct Path to Realization, Windhorse, 2003, pp. 237–8*

[74] Guy Claxton,: *The Heart of Buddhism,* Thorson, 1992, p. 64; pp. 105–120

[75] Nyanatiloka: *Buddhist Dictionary,* 3rd Edition, The Buddha Educational Foundation, Taiwan, 1970, p.26

[76] Sangharakshita: op. cit, p.75

[77] Ratnaprabha: 'Sowing seeds in the soil of the mind – The Alaya', June 23, 2018, www.alaya.thebuddhistcentre.com

[78] Chogyam Trungpa: *Training the Mind and Cultivating Loving-Kindness,* Shambhala,1993, p.21; Pema Chodron: *Start Where You Are,* Element / Harper Collins, 2003, p.21

[79] Rigdzin Shikpo: *Openness Clarity Sensitivity,* Longchen Foundation, 2000, pp.13–15; p.21; p.27.
In the *'Tathagatagarbha Sutta'* the Buddha Mind is presented by means of a sequence of images, such as a gold trinket encrusted with mud or a treasure buried beneath a hovel. But

the process whereby the owner comes to know of this hidden wealth is not clear, so I prefer Rigdzin Shikpo's version. See *The Tathagatagarbha Sutta*, in Donald Lopez (Ed): *Buddhism in Practice*, University of Princeton Press, 1995, pp. 92–106.

[80] Paul Gilbert: *The Compassionate Mind,* Constable, 2010, pp.116–21

[81] Carl Jung: 'On the Concept of the Archetype', in *Four Archetypes,* Routledge, 2003, pp. 7–14

[82] Sangharakshita: op.cit, p.43

[83] Carl Jung: *The Integration of the Personality,* Kegan Paul, 1940, pp. 20–21

[84] Frederic Jameson: *The Political Unconscious,* Routledge, 1981, p.34

[85] See Claude Levi-Strauss: *Structural Anthropology,* Penguin, 1972, pp. 233–9

[86] www.themindfulnessinitiative.org

[87] www. Meet the Mindfulness Caucus: Politicians Who meditate!

[88] Robert Booth: 'Way Ahead of the Curve' *The Guardian,* October, 13th, 2017

[89] www. Stop, Think, Breathe...Vote: Mindfulness in Parliament.

[90] www. How Meditation Benefits CEOs

[91] www. Meditation Awareness Training (MAT) for Work-related Well-being and Job Performance

[92] Prayudh Payutto: *Buddhadamma: Natural Laws and Values for Life*, State University of New York Press, 1995, pp.223–4

[93] Jon Kabat-Zinn: *Full Catastrophe Living*, Delta, 1990, p.424

[94] Steven Laureys and Helen Thomas: 'Meditation can help with covid-19 anxiety', *New Scientist,* April 3rd, 2021, p.10

[95] Thomas Armstrong: *Mindfulness in the Classroom,* ASCD (Association for Supervision and Curriculum Development), 2019, p.10; pp.15–16; p.55

[96] Thomas Armstrong: op.cit, p.118; Chapter 9

[97] Thomas Armstrong: op. cit, pp. 119–120

[98] Thomas Armstrong: op. cit, p.66

[99] Clive Erricker & Jane Erricker (Eds.): *Meditation in Schools*, Continuum, 2001, pp. 35–7

[100] Clive Erricker & Jane Erricker (Eds.): op. cit, p. 142

[101] See Dhivan Thomas Jones: *This Being, That Becomes: The Buddha's Teaching on Conditionality,* Windhorse, 2011, p.156

[102] Dhivan Thomas Jones: op.cit, pp. 5–6

[103] Alasdair MacIntyre: *After Virtue: A Study in Moral Theory,* 2nd Edition, Duckworth, 1985, p.59

[104] Alasdair MacIntyre: op.cit, p.58

[105] Alasdair MacIntyre: op.cit, p.12

[106] Alasdair MacIntyre: op.cit, p.64; p.6

[107] Alasdair MacIntyre: op.cit, p. 184

[108] Aristotle: *Ethics,* Revised Edition, Penguin, 1986, p.90; p.104; p.160

[109] Nyanatiloka: *Buddhist Dictionary,* 3rd Edition, The Buddha Educational Foundation, Taiwan, 1970, (p.94)

[110] See Aristotle: op.cit, p.91; Alasdair MacIntyre: op.cit., p.184

[111] Bikkhu Analayo: *Mindfulness of Breathing,* Windhorse, 2019, p. 6

[112] Bikkhu Analayo: op. cit., p.7

[113] Shunryu Susuki: *Zen Mind, beginners Mind,* Weatherhill, 1999, p. 25; p.28

[114] They are usually called 'hindrances'. See Bikkhu Bodhi (Ed): *In the Buddha's Words,* Wisdom, 2005, pp. 270–2.

[115] Santideva: *A Guide to the Bodhhisattva Way of Life,* Snow Lion, 1997, Chapter V, verse 3

[116] Bikkhu Bodhi (Ed): op.cit, p. 240

[117] Thich Nath Hanh: *Breathe! You Are Alive,* Rider, 1992, p.20

[118] Shorter Oxford English Dictionary, Third Edition. (Emphasis added)

[119] Vishvapani Blomfield: *Gautama Buddha,* Quercus, 2012, p. 216

[120] Sangharakshita: *Living With Awareness,* Windhorse, 2003, p.74ff

[121] 'The Observance Day', in *The Udana: Inspired Utterances of the Buddha,* 5.5, Buddhist Publication Society, 1997, p.74

Milton Keynes UK
Ingram Content Group UK Ltd.
UKHW020736191123
432823UK00012BA/271

9 781398 471924